T0289522

Sometimes I'm Happy

Sometimes I'm Happy

A WRITER'S MEMOIR

Marshall Sprague

Swallow Press
Ohio University Press
ATHENS

Swallow Press / Ohio University Press, Athens, Ohio 45701
© Copyright 1995 by Marshall Sprague
Printed in the United States of America
All rights reserved

99 98 97 96 95   5 4 3 2

Swallow Press / Ohio University Press books
are printed on acid-free paper ∞

Library of Congress Cataloging-in-Publication Data

Sprague, Marshall.
     Sometimes I'm happy : a writer's memoir / Marshall Sprague.
          p.   cm.
     ISBN 0–8040–0986–4
     1. Sprague, Marshall.   2. Historians—United States—
Biography.   I. Title.
E175.5.S78A3   1995
973'.07202—dc20
     [B]   94–37443
                                                              CIP

THIS BOOK IS FOR EDNA JANE, MY LUCKY STAR.

Contents

(photo section follows page 120)

Chapter One

"Round on the End"

S O WENT the riddle that my sister Josie and I sang through our Ohio childhood.

> You can find it on the map,
> Look both high and low—
> Round on the end and high in the middle.
> Ohio! That's the riddle!"

I was born in 1909 on a dreary, rainy March morning in the so-called "yellow room" of the old Sprague home in the pleasant Ohio town of Newark near the center of the state between Columbus and Zanesville. Though I left Newark after graduating from Princeton in 1930 for newspaper work elsewhere, I never outgrew attitudes that I acquired as a child in Newark and that greatest of American states, Ohio. Years later as I gazed at Notre Dame in Paris my rapture was the same rapture that I had experienced on a hot summer day gazing at the blue, blue Ohio sky above Newark. I still have my Ohio drawl and I still say "hell's afire" when something astonishes me. (I am easily astonished.) I think often of my years in Newark with affection and gratitude. In later travels I found that one's home town is the one place where one knows which way is north.

In 1909, Newark was a stable, tranquil, fairly prosperous town of twenty thousand people, some of whom were well-read and had travelled widely. Newark's wide East and West Main street met at a tree-lined square containing the Licking County Courthouse topped by an ornate tower with a clock that chimed on the hour. Newark was founded a year before Ohio became in 1803 the first state to be created in the Northwest Territory. The oldest Ohio town down on the Ohio River was Marietta (1788) named for the Queen of France, Marie Antoinette, because France had owned Ohio before 1763. Chillicothe was Ohio's first capital (1803). Newark people had wanted their town to be the capital but Zanesville beat them to it in 1810. Because of Zanesville's priority, the Sprague family was forever jealous of Zanesville and passed their jealousy on to me. Columbus was a brand new town created out of empty land in 1812 to be Ohio's capital.

My grandfather, Henry Day Sprague, was born in 1817 in Cooperstown, New York. In 1830 he rode a barge from Cleveland down to Newark on the Ohio and Erie Canal which had just been opened all the way through the interior of Ohio to Portsmouth on the Ohio River above Cincinnati. As the Ohio historian Walter Havighurst wrote, "This canal irradiated Ohio like a summer sunrise." It put Newark and the villages along the towpath of the canal—Akron, Massillon, Dover, Coshocton and Chillicothe—on national water routes of commerce. The first dirt for the canal was dug in 1825 at its high point, near Newark, which was nicknamed "the canal capital of Ohio." To serve the barge crews Newark became a boom town of saloons, dance halls and parlor houses—"Gingerbread Row" along the Canal Street towpath. Most of these happy sin enterprises closed down when the Pennsylvania and B. & O. railroads reached Newark in 1850. Thereafter, on any day Newark was a model of righteousness, with only occasional lapses.

My grandfather Henry Day taught himself enough law to pass the Ohio bar exam. In 1846, he married a Newark girl, Elizabeth Taylor, and started building our home a block from the town square and the Licking County Courthouse. All five of the children of Henry Day Sprague and Elizabeth Taylor—my future relatives—were born in the big upstairs "yellow room" well before the start of the Civil War. My Aunt Fanny was born in 1846; Aunt Mary (1849); Uncle George (1851); Uncle Hal (1857); and my father Joseph Taylor Sprague (1860). Though these relatives came out of the long ago, I never thought of them as old. I would find in me some characteristic of each of them as I developed. My grandfather died in 1897 leaving an estate of nearly $100,000. That was the usual size of an estate for Newark's older families—the Buckinghams, Fleeks, Wrights and Robbins—who had prospered as Newark grew from a tiny village to a city. Henry Day's estate was distributed to his five children by his executor, my Aunt Mary, a serenely authoritative lady who by common consent managed the affairs of all the Spragues. Aunt Mary never had to explain why she was in charge of everybody. She just *was*.

———

In 1900 Joseph Taylor, who became my father, reached his fortieth year—always a distressing milestone for men. He had never married, feeling that he was a poor catch compared to his smart older brothers. George Sprague had attended Cornell University. He was the town's wit and much in demand to speak at Elk's Club banquets. He had the gumption to start the Sprague Grocery Company in the 1880s, hiring his pliant younger brother Joe to run it at a low wage while he spent his time as president in and out of the store—but mostly out, being absorbed in the important business of making money at which he excelled.

Hal Sprague graduated from Yale in 1881 with a degree in architecture. My father Joe, the neglected younger son, was not pushed by his father beyond grade school and McGuffey readers. In Chicago after Yale, Hal Sprague had tinkered with an idea for a workable meter to measure gas consumption, foreseeing gas as the future fuel for heating homes instead of coal. He perfected and patented his Sprague meter in 1895 and set up in Bridgeport, Connecticut, with a loan of $40,000 from his roommate at Yale, William Phelps Eno, a wealthy New Yorker. Hal's Sprague Meter is standard in homes to this day. You may have one in your home.

At Yale, Uncle Hal became fond of dressing in the latest style. Meanwhile my father Joe never cared about his clothes, wearing a suit until it nearly fell off him.

Though Joe Sprague kept putting off marriage into the start of the twentieth century, his celibate years were to end soon. The cause of his change of heart was the daily passage by his office at Sprague Grocery of an auburn-haired nineteen-year-old girl named Della Cochran as she walked home from teaching in her one-room school in the "Texas" part of south Newark. As she passed Joe's window, Della sometimes smiled at Joe who would smile respectfully in return. And so the two of them exchanged these guileless smiles until one day Joe

Sprague found himself possessed by a wild idea. He would ask that pretty creature Della Cochran to marry him. With her as his wife, he would put his wasted bachelor years behind him and find fulfillment at last.

In later years, I learned of Della Cochran's background from my older sister Josie. She was born in 1881 on a farm near Coshocton. Her father deserted his wife and two small children when Della was ten years old. Her heroic mother Louisa Cochran moved with her children to live in East Newark on the wrong side of the Pennsylvania Railroad tracks. Louisa endured years of desperate poverty supporting her children by taking in the washing of Newark's upper crust on Hudson Avenue which Della delivered. Louisa's struggle ended in 1900 when she married a widowed farmer, James Osburn and moved to his forty-acre farm in London Hollow four miles east of Newark. Meanwhile, the teen-aged Della Cochran wangled a job—she was an expert wangler—teaching school in the "Texas" part of South Newark. Some of her pupils were older and twice as big as she was. Along with her teaching Della displayed unusual talent as a self-taught pianist. She became organist for Newark's Baptist Church. And so when Joe Sprague began smiling at the twenty-year-old Della Cochran she was quite well known in Newark for her musicianship and her beauty.

The courtship of Joe and Della was a quiet affair—buggy rides to Horn's Hill, ice cream socials, rides to Flint Ridge for the scenery, or trips on the interurban to the amusement park at Buckeye Lake. Four years passed before Della decided that she could do without heady romance and be happy with a husband twenty years older than she was. She did not pretend that she was in love with Joe. But she was fond of him—his courtly old-fashioned ways, his quaint humor, his honesty. She knew Joe would never be a rich man like his brother George. But Della believed that by becoming one of the old Newark family of Spragues, (even if they ignored her socially) she would be spared the heart-breaking poverty that she had known with her mother as a child. She knew that Joe loved her and was proud of her talents and her beauty. She could count on Joe to stand by her in her determination to show the world that the poor unschooled farm girl from Coshocton could amount to something.

Della and Joe were married on Christmas Day, 1903. Della was not pleased with Joe's decision that because of his low salary at the grocery, they would live with his fifty-seven-year-old sister Mary in the old Sprague home at 25 First Street, which he said was big enough for the three of them. The stately Mary Sprague was the most highly esteemed woman in Newark. Della felt uneasy in her presence but found her pleasant enough though Mary Sprague made it clear in her kindly way that she was in charge of affairs on First Street.

On Halloween in 1903 the following October, my sister Josie was born in the "yellow room," the birth place of so many Spragues. My father had hoped for a boy to be named Joe. He comforted his wife. "Never mind, Della. We'll call her Josephine. She's a pretty little goblin. We'll keep her."

For several years, harmony prevailed in the dual Sprague household. On March 14, 1909, our jovial physician Dr. Rank ushered me in to the world. After he had assured my beautiful egocentric mother, aged twenty-eight, that the birthing had gone well, he congratulated my father, now aged forty-nine, for siring the first male Sprague of his generation. Perhaps Dr. Rank told Joe Sprague with a wink that not many men of his advanced years had the virility and the sex appeal to produce a son.

Soon after my birth, my Aunt Mary and Uncle George came to look me over and to name me. I was a sorry sight—a fat, torpid baby (I weighed ten pounds at birth) without hair or eyebrows, and unable to hold up my head, all of which supported my mother's prediction that I must be retarded. Uncle George proposed that I be named "Marshall" in honor of the first Supreme Court Justice of the United States, John Marshall.

And so I came to be Marshall Taylor Sprague. I always rather liked my name. I felt it had a nice distinguished flow to it—like "Henry Wadsworth Longfellow." But when in 1931 I got my first newspaper job in New York at *Women's Wear Daily* my copy desk man Sam Friedman told me that my full name was too long for a by-line. I dropped the "Taylor" though I did not achieve the distinction of a by-line until 1933 when I was a reporter for the *North China Star* in Tientsin, China.

At age two I could hold up my head, but I worried my mother with all of a child's minor ailments though I escaped scarlet fever which would have brought those fearsome red quarantine posters at front doors barring entrance into that house. In addition to Della Sprague's worries about me, she suffered the frustrations of an ambitious, attractive young woman married to a husband old enough to be her father which, in fact, best describes Joe Sprague's relation to his wife Della.

During my infancy a bone of contention arose between my mother and the older Spragues. The conflict had its origin when my Aunt Mary heard that her sister Fanny Sprague (my aunt born in 1846) was ill. She asked Della to go to New York to check on her condition.

This Fanny had always been the rebel in the Sprague family. She had fled from Newark in the 1870s to escape the uprightness of her sister Mary. In New York Fanny learned Gregg shorthand, got a job as a secretary, bobbed her hair, campaigned for female suffrage, free love, abortion and the right of women to smoke cigars, wear bloomers and enter saloons unattended. She supported Victoria Woodhull and her equal rights candidacy for President of the United States.

In the 1900s, Fanny Sprague adopted a life style of dubious propriety in New York and Paris with a lover or two. She began drinking too much. This had prompted Mary Sprague to have her committed to a drying-out hospital in the Adirondacks. Fanny broke out of the hospital and resumed her unseemly conduct in New York which was why Mary Sprague sent her sister-in-law Della Sprague from Newark to New York to see what could be done for Fanny.

Now in her sixties, Fanny Sprague greeted Della warmly in her small apartment house on West 104th Street which she had built with money from the Henry Day Sprague estate. The two women took to each other at once with much laughter over the stuffy ways of the Newark Spragues. Della was entranced with the things she learned from the worldly Fanny Sprague—how to smoke cigarettes, how to mix cocktails, how to dress, how to avoid pregnancy. Fanny arranged an evening for Della with her old friend and lawyer, Alexander Thane, who took her to dinner at the Waldorf Astoria.

A few weeks after Della returned to Newark from New York, she received a letter from Alexander Thane. He wrote that Fanny Sprague had died suddenly. Enclosed in his letter was a copy of the will he had drawn up for Fanny before her death. The will bequeathed her apartment house at 126 West 104th Street to Della.

News of this bequest was received by George and Mary Sprague with restrained indignation. Mary Sprague remarked that when she sent Della to New York she did not dream that Fanny would give to a non-Sprague property that belonged in the family since Fanny had bought it with her inheritance from Henry Day Sprague. The two Spragues did not mention their view of Fanny's will to Joe, assuming that he would agree with their superior judgment as usual.

But one day at a Sunday supper (as Josie told me later), George Sprague made an oblique reference to Fanny's disloyal act. To the surprise of George and Mary, Joe stood up. "George," he said, "and you, too, Mary. It was Fanny's dying wish that Della inherit her New York apartment house. I don't want to hear another word from either of you about it."

———

I recall little of my early childhood in Newark. Our parents took very good care of Josie and me. But they were not enthusiastic parents. Mother was deeply involved in her musical ambitions. My father was not physically up to the incessant athletics of his young children. Outdoor picnics were not much fun because of our mother's horror of ants. Christmas at our house passed without a candle-lit tree. It would never have occurred to my father on Christmas Eve to prance in costume pretending to be Santa Claus. I remember my dismay one Christmas when I longed for an electric train. Instead my father gave me an oatmeal dish with yellow ducks galloping around it. Mother's present was equally dismal—a round celluloid Buster Brown collar for me to wear when I recited for mother's friends—"Bobby Shaftoe went to sea, silver buckles on his knee." Much as I disliked the collar, I did my best to put Bobby Shaftoe over because I was born with Uncle George's exhibitionist streak and liked to be applauded.

In 1915, my Aunt Mary, now aged sixty-six, returned to Newark after one of her extensive trips to Europe. During her absence, Joe Sprague moved his family to the nearby Sherwood Hotel while the old First Street home with its many fireplaces and sizzling gas-mantle lights was modernized with central gas heating, electric lights, two bathrooms and a crank-to-ring telephone. The old, tastefully built, brick privy in the back yard was boarded up for Josie and me to use as a play house.

The big remodelled house was divided in two of everything—sixteen large rooms, two living and dining rooms and two kitchens, separate front doors and two side porches. Josie told me that the house was divided because our mother refused to share the old house any longer with Mary Sprague. Della, Josie said, was tired of having her life arranged however subtly by my Aunt Mary as she was accustomed to arrange the affairs of her many admirers.

I asked Josie why Aunt Mary was treated by everybody as though she were the Queen of England. "Why, Marsh," Josie said, "didn't you know that Aunt Mary wrote a book once?" She went on to explain that her book was a novel titled provocatively *An Earnest Trifler*. The action of it was set in the White Mountains of New England where Aunt Mary had never been. The plot was about two men passionately in love with the same girl. Josie and I could not imagine that Aunt Mary had ever been in love. She wrote the novel, it would seem, out of the imaginings of a thirty-year-old spinster. She sent the novel to a book man born in Ohio, William Dean Howells, who was editor then of *The Atlantic Monthly*. Howells passed it on to the editor of Houghton Osgood, the Boston publisher. Osgood liked the novel and published it in 1879.

The novel turned out to be huge success with a sale of sixty thousand copies. The royalties from the book's sale permitted Mary Aplin Sprague of Newark, Ohio, to finance her first trip to Europe.

As the best-selling author of 1879, Mary Sprague became a national celebrity overnight. To promote her novel, her publisher brought her to Boston to be guest of honor at breakfast with Oliver Wendell Holmes on his seventy-first birthday. Others at the breakfast included Henry Wadsworth Longfellow, Ralph Waldo Emerson and Thomas Bailey Aldrich. Later Mary Sprague was invited to a birthday party in Boston for Harriet Beecher Stowe.

I reacted to all this exciting news about Aunt Mary by saying to Josie, "Do you mean to tell me that all Aunt Mary had to do to become famous and have everybody in Newark treat her like royalty was to write a book a long time ago? Well, then, I am going to be a writer when I grow up."

Chapter Two

A Boy's Life in Ohio

— 1917 —

THE JOE SPRAGUES had their half of the remodelled First Street house down our alley from the Newark Square; Aunt Mary had her half. But the big house had eight doors connecting the two parts. Aunt Mary did not lock any of them so I had the run of the whole place. My private domain was the big closet under our stairway. I marked it with Josie's lipstick: "Keep Out! Signed Green Top the DWARFF."

My bedroom upstairs was between Dad's and Mother's room. Mother turned out my light at 9 P.M., but there was an electric light in my clothes closet. I could read there undisturbed (I read quite well at age seven). I read those delightful stories of Thornton Burgess—"The Adventures of Jimmy Skunk" and "Old Mother West Wind." After dark I could step from my bedroom through my window to our kitchen porch and climb down the grape trellis to our backyard where I pretended that I was Robin Hood in Sherwood Forest fooling the law (my parents) by robbing the rich to give to the poor.

Before falling asleep in bed, I enjoyed the rattle of the ten pins toppling in the bowling alley across from the Auditorium Theatre down our alley. I decided to get a job setting up pins on the way to becoming a writer. One night I heard from the Auditorium the Highlands brogue of Sir Harry Lauder singing during his annual show in Newark.

My second sanctuary was on the large third floor of our attic with its lovely smell of oak rafters and Aunt Mary's leather round-topped trunks with her faded tourist labels still on them—"Hotel Nettuna, Pisa"; "Ye Olde Hop Pole, Cambridge"; "Hotel Royal, Sorrento"; "Prague"; "Dresden." Through a small attic window, I could get to the slate roof of our house with its steep gullies and high ridges which I thought must be like Pikes Peak as described by my third grade teacher, Miss Beecher.

In Aunt Mary's big front hall, there was an iron umbrella stand built to catch the drip of rain from visitors' umbrellas. If I was in a hurry to go I would drip myself at the umbrella stand until Etta Shea, Aunt Mary's Irish cook, caught me at it and that ended my dripping. I thought that Aunt Mary was too dignified and feeble to punish my frequent misconduct. But one day she saw me sticking my finger in our uncovered baseboard electric outlet for the thrill of the sharp electric shock. Aunt Mary pounced on me, flung me to the floor and sat on me until I promised never to run the risk of electrocuting myself again.

Most of Newark's well-to-do residents had left the congested Square area where we lived to build uptown on fashionable Hudson Avenue or Granville Street. I liked living downtown because I saw interesting things there that children uptown never saw. My downtown playmate was George Shawl. His mother, George told me, had a "sort of business." She served tea to Baltimore & Ohio brakemen in her cottage behind the Sherwood Hotel. Sister Josie told me that Mrs. Shawl wore "button-up" shoes like those worn by ladies strolling on Canal Street near "Gingerbread Row." I gathered that such shoes signified something unmentionable. But then I noted "button-up" shoes were worn by society ladies attending the "Monday Talks" which Aunt Mary had organized for intellectual discussion. Looking back, I am sure that Joe Sprague knew about Mrs. Shawl's "business" of serving tea to B. & O. brakemen. My father always put people in the best possible light. When I told him Mrs. Shawl's husband lived out of town, Dad said, "Oh, yes, George Shawl. He's a famous Irish playwright. Lives in Pittsburgh."

I walked down our alley daily and around the Square past the Park National Bank, the Greek ice cream place (gigantic banana splits) and Tommy Evans' drug store. At Diment's coffee shop I might find George Hoster's low-slung convertible Stutz Bearcat (George played on the Pure Oil Twilight League baseball team). I would stop in the Bazaar Saloon for the baseball scores chalked on the blackboard behind the bar as they came in from Western Union. Children were not allowed in the Bazaar but the bartender let me watch the scores because Uncle George owned the building.

My main interest in our short alley was the huge cylindrical fire escape of the Auditorium Theatre. It rose up to exit doors on the second and third floor balconies. In case of fire, the audience could step inside the cylinder and slide down the iron chute to safety in our alley. I managed to pry open the door at the bottom of the chute and climb up to the unlocked exit door into the third floor balcony. I saw my first stage show via the chute—"Peck's Bad Boy." My second stolen show was "The Passing Show." I was stunned when four chorus girls appeared on the stage topless with roses fastened to their nipples. Without being specific my parents led me to believe that ladies did not display their nipples in public.

On my eighth birthday Dad gave me my first bicycle equipped with a New Departure coaster brake. Soon I learned how to get towed on my bicycle by hanging onto the rear of trucks. One day I was being towed by the truck of our vegetable man, Joe Martinella. Joe stopped his truck and backed up with me on my bike behind. I jumped clear but my beautiful new bike was crumpled by the truck's wheels. Joe took me home weeping. I told my Mother—"It was not Joe's fault!" Mother phoned Dad at the grocery about my mishap. An hour later Dad came with a new bike which he was able to buy at a discount because the frame was bent a little. But I found that the bent bike rode well if I leaned a little to compensate for the bend. I was grateful to Dad for buying that second bike. It removed from my memory that Christmas when Dad gave me the cereal bowl with the galloping ducks.

My bicycle extended my range in Newark beyond the Square and 25 First Street. The city was surrounded by corn and wheat farms in the lush valley of the Licking River which joined the Muskingum River at Horn's Hill. That hill and others around town were foothills of the Allegheny Mountains in Pennsylvania.

East and West Main Street met at the Square. From there Newark lay two miles north up Hudson Avenue past the bottle works and the water treatment plant. Twenty-five miles north was Mount Vernon and Kenyon College. West of the Square was Wehrle stove factory and the Moundbuilders Country Club. The Country Club's nine-hole golf course was plotted around sixteen-foot high mounds built by prehistoric "Red Paint" Indians. I spent two summers caddying at Moundbuilders at twenty-five cents a round. The golfers had their names stamped on their golf balls and if I found somebody's lost ball I was given fifteen cents for it. Each tee had a sand box and a bucket of water where I could scrub my golfer's ball and set his ball on sand tees (wooden tees were unknown then).

The low Indian mounds were a problem for golfers at Moundbuilders. My job as a caddy was to stand on top of a mound and give my golfer the line from his ball over my head to the hole hidden behind the mound, being careful to duck if his approach shot came at me. Seven miles west of the country club was the charming village of Granville, a bit of transplanted New England. Granville was the seat of Denison University (1832).

South from Newark Square was the Sprague Grocery warehouse located on Canal Street and an unfilled portion of the old barge canal. Below Canal Street and the Pennsylvania Railroad tracks, better known as the "Pennsy," was the "Texas" part of South Newark and the high bluff of the Catholic Cemetery. Ten miles further south the road reached Jacktown and the National Road, the historic first federal highway running through Columbus to Indianapolis. The National Road ran near Buckeye Lake where Dad had a farm which he had inherited from Henry Day Sprague. If I rode my bike east from the Square I would pass the Heisey Glassware plant and Cedar Hill Cemetery which held the graves of my grandparents, my great-grandparents and my Aunt Fanny. Out East Main Street I passed the brick buildings of the Newark orphanage. From the orphanage the Zanesville interurban tracks ran past Swan's Blacksmith and the gravel road which led to Grandmother Osburn's farm.

By 1917, the gossips in Newark knew well that the Spragues on First Street were not getting along very well. They blamed this on the independence my Mother had achieved when she inherited Aunt Fanny's New York apartment house, which gave her an income of as much as $75 a month. She could do things with that money on her own. Dad could not be budged further from Newark than Buckeye Lake, so Mother took Josie and me one summer to Oak Bluffs in Martha's Vineyard. She saved up $1,700 and bought a Steinway parlor grand piano. She went to New York to collect the rent from the apartments and to study piano at Aeolian Hall with Walter Damrosch. She became president of the Newark Music Club. She found a concert agent in New York, Charles N. Drake, who specialized in supplying musicians such as Josef Hoffman and Fritz Kreisler for concerts in small towns.

Thinking of me as the child of a broken home, my First Street neighbors treated me with kindly concern. Isabel Skinner across the street plied me with dishes of rice pudding which I hated. But I was unaware that I was an unfortunate child. Both of my parents spoiled me to compensate for their marital difficulties. Dad did not punish me when the police hauled me off for breaking into the Episcopalian rectory next door in search of cookies.

Whatever her problems, my mother did not neglect me. She lulled me to sleep by playing Chopin preludes on her Steinway. She read to me Stevenson's *Treasure Island* and *A Child's Garden of Verses*. I loved Kipling's *Just So Stories* especially "The Cat That Walked by Himself." Mother studied child care articles in *McCall's Magazine* which recommended that children smoke Benson and Hedges cigarettes to show their independence. A *McCall's* article persuaded Mother to send me to Newark's Christian Science Sunday School. I quit the school explaining to Mother that I found Jesus Christ much more interesting than Mary Baker Eddy.

I appreciated my Mother's care of me though I felt at times that I was competing for her affection with her Steinway.

But I enjoyed my father because he was so interesting. At age sixty Joseph Taylor was a handsome, slender man, five feet nine inches tall, with a Roman nose, a small moustache, and the sort of kindly face that made his friends eager to tell him their troubles. He shaved with a straight razor and often cut himself because he never quite got the hang of it. He was a terrible driver of our 1913 Oldsmobile. He never knew what gear he was in and sometimes backed the Oldsmobile into a tree. He never used profanity. But if he picked up a stranger on the road, his small talk became full of cuss words to show the stranger that he was a regular guy.

Dad was so kind to me. I became hysterical whenever Mother tried to make me take castor oil. Dad would come and gulp down half a bottle of the stuff—smacking his lips with pleasure. I got the shivers in the morning watching Dad take a cold water bath. Perhaps he got the habit in childhood during the Civil War when hot water bathrooms were unknown. Mother would not let Dad smoke or chew Mail Pouch tobacco. But he got around her by chewing cigars to pieces without smoking them.

Joe Sprague was slow to react to crises. Our backyard garage caught fire one night. The horse-drawn fire truck rushed in with bells clanking.

A hundred neighbors came to put it out. In the morning I rushed to tell Dad. I found he had slept through all the commotion. He looked out his window, saw nothing burning, muttered "Gad!" and went back to bed. I noticed one morning that Dad differed from me in that he had not been circumcised. I asked Aunt Mary to tell me the reason for Dad's peculiar structure. The virginal Aunt Mary had probably never seen the structure. She turned beet red and fled the room.

I had happy times with Joe Sprague. We attended Barnum and Bailey's Circus with passes he got for grocery discounts. Mother was scared of elephants and would not go to the circus. It was ritual in late October for Dad and me to put the Oldsmobile up for the winter. I helped Dad drain the radiator as antifreeze was unknown. The air-cooled Franklin of our Episcopal minister next door was the one car in Newark that was driven all winter.

Dad treated his Oldsmobile and everything else animate and in-animate—like an old friend. To keep the Oldsmobile cozy and warm he insulated the garage walls with big Kellogg Corn Flakes cartons. When March came we had the excitement of taking the Olds off its jacks, filling the radiator and priming the carburetor. Dad would start cranking, with the crank halfway upside so that the crank would not break his arm if the motor backfired. Tense moments for both of us. And then, the motor would cough, spit out a lot of primer smoke from the exhaust and start. Hallelujah!

My father did not care for golf. On his first try, his mid-iron shot hit and killed a robin. In sorrow, he quit golf. His favorite sport was swimming. He had a homemade cabin on his Buckeye Lake farm that he built with Napoleon Smith, his Sprague Grocery foreman. Pole worked on the cabin for nothing because Dad always bailed him out of jail when he was locked up for too much drinking. At the Buckeye Lake cabin, Dad would swim out a mile from shore and paddle around for hours like a contented frog.

———

When George Shawl and his mother left Newark and moved to Columbus, my new friend was Billy Korn. Billy and I stole chocolate bars from Sprague Grocery and shells for my .22 rifle which I bought with money earned from caddying at Moundbuilders Country Club. Billy and I had just discovered girls. After supper we would ride our bikes past the front porches of several girls who waited for us on their porch swings. We would greet them if no parents were in sight, otherwise we hurried on.

In summer Billy and I sold pop at a table in front of his house. Coca-Cola had not reached Newark yet. Our best seller was an orange drink called "Whistle" with the logo "Just Whistle." Billy and I went swimming out Hudson Avenue past the victory gardens (of World War I) to the swimming hole near the water works dam. The two of us enjoyed staring at the grown-up girls at the dam.

We stared specially at Aileen Martin whose father was Dad's dentist. Aileen's skirted bathing suit tried hard to hold all of her in. After staring at Aileen we stared at Mary Ellis, the daughter of Aunt Mary's favorite grocer, Hugh Ellis. The charms Billy and I noted in these two girls were to be confirmed later. Aileen spent two years in the chorus of the Vincent Youmans musical, "No, No, Nanette." Mary Ellis, a soprano, starred with Dennis King in "Rose Marie."

I learned about sex as we all do—from other children since parents cannot bring themselves to describe it. One day Billy and I rode our bikes across the Indiana Street bridge and leaned over the railing to watch the sunfish skittering around in the Licking River below. Billy said, "Marsh, do you know how babies are born?" I had to admit that nobody had told me. Billy went on to say that his sister had told him all about it—where this went and that went and why.

I couldn't believe my ears. "But Billy, wouldn't I have to take my clothes off to do all that?" I asked.

"Of course," Billy said, "don't be dumb."

"Hell's afire! I'd be too embarrassed to be naked in front of girls."

So I had my first lesson in life's most intriguing and universal activity.

By 1918, my mother was spending more and more time away from Newark studying in New York to become a concert pianist. In her absences I often stayed with Grandma and my step-grandfather on the Osburn farm. I would take my rifle, a sandwich and a bottle of Whistle and ride past Cedar Hill Cemetery and out a back road past the Glaumsinger's wheat thresher, and the Pigg farm where the girl lived who went after me with a buggy whip when I called her what she was—a redhead. Just before Grandma's was the farm of a man who trained pacers for sulky races at the Newark fair grounds.

Grandma and Granddad Osburn lived well back from the road in a square white house with a New England-style widow's walk on top. A windmill pumped water to the water tank in Grandma's kitchen which had a waterback for hot water in the big stove. A handsome coal-oil lamp hung over the dining room table. A cuckoo clock with a bird that popped out on the hour was near the telephone where Grandma spent time chatting with her neighbors on the party line. The Osburn privy was beyond the wood house—it was a two-holer with a low hole for children.

On arriving at the Osburns I would take off my town clothes and put on my overalls. Then I would run barefoot through the Osburn wheat field to find the Shaner boys on their farm below the Osburns. I admired Mr. Shaner because he grew ginseng which he shipped to Manchuria where the Chinese chewed the roots to increase their potency.

Playing with the Shaner boys was more fun than playing in Newark. We would make tunnels through the Shaner straw shack in crisscross patterns so that if lost we could be found by boys using other tunnels. We battled bumblebees. We cornered copperhead snakes. We pretended that we were Buffalo Bill tracking hostile Indians. If we spotted another boy we peppered him with shots from our .22 rifles—aiming low enough above his head so that the whir of the bullet would remind an "Indian" to hold still and submit to capture.

My Grandma Osburn was a serene, fun-loving lady—quite unlike her daughter, my serious mother, so preoccupied with her ambitions. I liked to watch Grandma milking her thirteen cows. I would help her carry the pails of fresh milk to the cellar and turn the handle of the Laval separator. Thin milk came out of the large spout and thick cream from the small spout.

Those were horse-and-buggy days at the Osburns though Granddad bought a "Tin Lizzy" in 1919 for $275. He had two wagon horses that he called Nancy Hanks and Dan Patch. He bought them from Sprague Grocery when the grocery went modern with a Model-T truck for deliveries. Granddad Osburn had a fifteen-year-old helper named John Lock from the Newark who taught me all the four-letter words he had picked up on the orphanage. I didn't know what they meant or how to pronounce them. One day I tried them on a rooster I was chasing in the Osburn chicken yard.

Unexpectedly, Granddad Osburn appeared. He told me to stop chasing his rooster. I drew myself up and spat out proudly, "Aw, shut up, you motha foggin' ole sonofa bitchin' bastard!"

To my dismay Granddad was not impressed by my cuss words. He grabbed me by the scruff of my neck and hauled me to stand before Grandma in the kitchen. Then he said, "I know, Marshall, where you learned those words. I'll talk to John Lock later. But if I ever hear you using them again I will send John back to the orphanage."

In all the years that have passed since, I feel Granddad's hand on my neck whenever I feel the urge to come out with four-letter words.

Chapter Three

MANHATTAN INTERIM

— 1919 —

I N THE EARLY FALL of 1918, I was spending a lot of time after school polishing buckeyes with spit in our backyard to give to Miss Beecher at Central School. In bed late one night I heard my parents talking downstairs. I got out of bed and sat down at the top of the stairs.

They were talking about a five-dollar hat that Mother had bought at Mazey's store and charged to Dad without his permission. Mother said that she would pay him for the hat. Then she went on to tell Dad that she had been saving rent money from Aunt Fanny's apartment house. She planned to leave Newark and go to New York for a year to study more piano at the Damrosch school. She wanted to take me with her and put me in school in New York. There was a pause and then I heard Dad say, "Do you want a divorce, Della?" At that, Mother began to sob.

I went back to bed. One by one my parents came up the stairs and into my room. Silently, each gave me a hug and a pat on the cheek.

Of course I was disturbed by what I had heard. But children (I was nine years old then) are resilient in facing up to bad news. Soon I was thinking about what fun it would be to go to New York. I would see the Woolworth Building and the Statue of Liberty!

All of us have unhappy memories. That night I wondered why my parents had decided to give themselves so much trouble over a five-dollar hat. I resolved not to be like them. I would arrange things to be happy—most of the time anyhow.

Well, since then I have had my fair share of happy days—marrying Edna Jane in 1939. EJ and I were happy about the birth of our first son, Joe, though in my enthusiasm about the birth I rushed to the wrong hospital to congratulate the mother. And there was the day in 1943 when I saw my first published book, *The Business of Getting Well.* And the day that same year when my T.B. doctor, Gerald Webb, told me in Colorado Springs I had "turned the corner." He meant by that that I would recover from tuberculosis.

I will never forget that fall evening in 1918 when I had my first ride on a Pullman car as Mother and I left Newark for New York. Dad took us to the station in the Oldsmobile to board the Pennsy's crack express train, the St. Louisan. (It was renamed "The Spirit of St. Louis" in 1927). I watched the train's big headlight appear as it came down the track from Columbus, smoke pouring from the stack of the locomotive, its whistle ah-ooing at Newark's street crossings. Our station platform shook as the engine's high drive wheels passed us and the thirteen-car Pullman train came to a screeching stop. The train's oilers dropped out of the coal car to check the cars for hot boxes.

Dad had bought upper and lower berths for us in the last Pullman car of the train. The porter had our step ready for us to climb aboard. We had no time for sad goodbyes when the conductor roared "All aboard!" As the train clanked into movement Dad yelled, "Stay awake, Marsh, past Pittsburgh. Watch for the Horseshoe Curve."

I learned a lot about Pullmans that night. Mother said that we had both berths which entitled us to sit facing forward in the double chair. Passengers with the cheaper upper berth had to sit riding backward. I loved the sooty smell of the car's upholstery.

I practiced the porter's stride in the swaying car with legs spread. In the aisle by the men's smoker I found a drinking place with paper cups and a roster of hotels approved by the Pennsy. I sat in the long seat of the smoking car by the window. With my Ingersoll watch I timed the speed of the train by counting the passage of telephone poles. Dad had told me that there were twenty-one telephone poles in each mile of track.

A drummer entered the smoker—he was like the drummers at Sprague Grocery. He brushed his teeth. For rinsing he used water from a push-button faucet. Then he took a towel from the rack and carefully swabbed the aluminum wash bowl. I resolved to do what the tidy drummer did when I brushed my teeth.

I was intrigued by the sign in the men's room urging me not to flush the toilet during train stops. I was glad I had not flushed it at the Trinway by-stop for Zanesville. Twenty years later I thought of Trinway when Edna Jane, my prom date at Princeton in 1929, sang to me to the tune of Dvorak's "Humoresque," the Vassar College ballad—"Passengers will please refrain from flushing toilets while the train is standing in the station, I love you."

The porter made up our berths. Mother took the windowless upper berth and gave me the lower with the window. I watched our stops at Coshocton, Newcomerstown and Steubenville. Nearing Pittsburgh I watched how the steel mill stacks set the night sky aflame. We coasted along the Ohio River past Pittsburgh. And then the locomotives strained to haul the train across the Allegheny Mountains. I was wide awake when the string of Pullmans moved around the four tracks of the Horseshoe Curve. I could see the locomotive and most of the train as it rounded the curve and stopped at Altoona. I don't think children ever forget that dramatic passage.

After breakfast we passed Trenton and Princeton Junction. Next I heard the porter announce "Lights out for three minutes while we go under the Hudson River." I wondered if the river would break through and drown us. We emerged safely from the tunnel into the sunlight of New York City and stopped at Pennsylvania Station.

The vastness of the station awed me and made me homesick for Newark's little depot far away. I hoped to get back to Newark to become a Tenderfoot in the Newark Boy Scouts. To buck myself up I stopped at a pop stand and asked for a bottle of Whistle. I was not pleased when the man said he had never heard of Newark's favorite pop.

Outside of Pennsylvania Station on 33rd Street, I forgot all about being homesick. Not far away I gazed at the Gothic beauty of the sixty-story Woolworth Building, the tallest in the world. Miss Beecher had told me that the building was a monument to the skill of Frank Woolworth in extracting the nickels and dimes that I spent at the five and ten in Newark. It would remain the world's tallest until the Chrysler Building (seventy-seven stories) went up in 1929. But to me the Woolworth is still the most beautiful of the city's many skyscrapers.

At the time in 1918 of my arrival in New York its four million residents were trying to get used to modernity. The Woolworth building was only five years old. Some people had not yet ridden on the West Side subway or the Columbus Avenue El. The subway gave them a ride for a nickel. The pie-shaped Flatiron Building was still a novelty. Tourists enjoyed the thrill of seeing the city from the open top deck of a Fifth Avenue bus. But the Brooklyn Bridge remained a marvel as did the Metropolitan Museum of Art and the Museum of Natural History.

Mother had hoped to live in one of her five apartments in her building on West 104th Street, but they were all occupied. So she rented two rooms at Janus Court on Morningside Drive. It was managed by Teachers College (part of Columbia). Mother learned that Teachers College administered Horace Mann Lower School on 120th Street near Janus Court. She enrolled me at Horace Mann, wangling a reduced tuition.

I found friends at Janus Court. The switchboard operator showed me how to run the switchboard and the elevator. In January two Chinese students at Columbia took me ice skating at the flooded Notlek tennis courts on Claremont Avenue near Grant's Tomb. The young Chinese showed me how to skate. Their kindness made me a lifelong admirer of the Chinese on into 1933 when I worked on a newspaper in China.

Mother had to economize in New York because her apartment rentals did not cover expenses. She found a cheap boarding house on Amsterdam Avenue. The meals were not as filling as Aunt Mary's, but the bread and butter were plentiful and I loaded up on them. The noise of people practicing on piano was not allowed at Janus Court. Mother rented a "dumb" piano—a soundless keyboard for finger practice.

Now and then, Mother left me alone while she had dinner with her old friend Charles Drake. Charlie had quit the concert business to manage the worldwide concerts of the violinist, Jascha Heifitz. I amused myself in Mother's absence at a card table at our window overlooking Morningside Park. Through the window I could see the passing El trains bound for Harlem. I pretended I was a train dispatcher. I kept a record of the express and local trains and wrote down the time of their passage. I pencilled push buttons on my time sheet. If the El trains seemed too close together I pushed the warning button to make the motorman slow down.

I enjoyed the two years I spent at Horace Mann. I learned to use tools in manual training. I was end man in our minstrel shows and hammed it up in my best Bobby Shaftoe style. I was pleased to be applauded in a gymnastic show for parents when I hurled myself in a somersault over eleven boys lying side by side on a canvas pad.

A Union Theological student took us on weekends across the Dyckman Street ferry to Fort Lee and into the empty park of the Palisades. We built fires and cooked hot dogs there. We found a cave with bats hanging in the ceiling. We activated the bats by striking kitchen matches below them. I enjoyed roller skating down Riverside Park along the Hudson River from Grant's Tomb to the Joan of Arc statue at 93rd Street. An anti-litter plaque by the statues impressed me. It read "Let no one say and say it to your shame, that all was beauty here until you came." I still think of that jingle and of Joan of Arc when I see a cigarette butt littering the sidewalk.

The spacing of the West Side subway stops was too much for Mother to remember. I memorized stops for her from the Bowery to Van Courtland Park. I learned how to follow the green guide line of the 42nd Street shuttle. I sometimes forgot to get off the Lenox Avenue Express at our 96th Street stop. The Lenox Avenue line dumped me up in the Bronx instead of 116th Street. On the subway I always went to the window of the front car to watch the tracks and the sparks from the third rail. Through a slit in the motorman's door I watched his hand on the throttle intending to pull the emergency stop cord if the motorman should fall asleep.

Mother tried her best to educate me culturally. She took me often to the Metropolitan Museum of Art. I especially admired the two thousand-year-old Egyptian mummy. As a Damrosch piano student Mother had passes to Carnegie Hall concerts. I listened dutifully to concerts by Paderewski, Misha Elman, and Rachmaninoff. I was more impressed by the singing of Kirsten Flagstad, Alma Gluck and Amelia Galli Curci, especially in their deathbed scenes.

My aesthetic feelings were nourished better when Mother took me to the Hippodrome. I watched with rapture as Charles Dillingam's girls in bathing suits walked down a long flight of stairs and marched rank on rank into a tank of water and disappeared. Another thing I liked in New York was the automat. I would walk along the line of little windows. At the apple pie window I would drop a dime in the slot, take out my pie and watch the appearance in my window of a replacement for the next apple pie lover.

In the winter of 1919 New York endured a record snowfall. On Amsterdam Avenue the street crews pushed the snow over to the gutters in piles fifteen feet high. I spent my indoor time that winter working on my plan to be a writer. I was fond of the poems of James Whitcomb Riley like "Knee Deep in June." I wrote reams of poems in what I hoped resembled Riley's homespun style. A sample of my style:

OUR COOK

Our cook (Her name is 'Liza Ann),
Is handy with her ol' dish pan,
Why she can make most any dish,
From fried eels to pickerel fish.

And oh! when Christmas comes around,
And I kill a turkey (Sure good meat),
And then into the kitchen I go,
To see what I will have to eat.

I sent one of my poems to the editor of *The St. Nicholas Magazine*. The kind-hearted editor sent me my first rejection slip. He wrote, "This is an interesting poem, but not quite suitable for us." Though I was rejected, that note convinced me that I was really a writer.

———

The people of New York have always enjoyed spectacles. Perhaps its greatest spectacle began in May 1919, when President Woodrow Wilson ordered most of the U.S. Navy into the Hudson River between the Statue of Liberty and Dyckman Street. Meanwhile General John J. Pershing, commander of the U.S. force in Europe, mustered out to Camp Upton thousands of doughboys and officers who had served in France. The eleven thousand men of New York's 77th Division commanded by Major General Robert Alexander and other units from twenty-six states were instructed to stage on May 3 a parade called "A Panorama of Victory" to run five miles down Fifth Avenue from 110th Street to Washington Square in Greenwich Village.

For weeks before the parades all of us at Horace Mann School wore big "Victory Bond" buttons and patrolled Riverside Drive taking pledges to buy bonds from people out on Riverside Drive to see the battleships floating on the Hudson.

May 3, 1919, was a cool sunny day as half a million people converged on New York and struggled to find places in the jammed wooden stands along Fifth Avenue. Part of Park Avenue above 50th Street was closed for use as headquarters for the bond sale. Mother had arranged for me to see the parade from a window of her dentist's office on Fifth Avenue at 49th Street.

I spent four hours at the dentist's window watching the passage of the "Panorama of Victory." Its floats presented in tableau form every aspect of life in France during World War I. One float showed soldiers building pontoon bridges. One showed Army nurses and doctors treating the wounded. Two French observation balloons were lashed to a truck with soldiers up in baskets to show how they observed the enemy. One float was full of pretty girls from Barnard and Hunter College representing French "farmerettes" serving coffee to front line soldiers in the Argonne.

One float had sides lined with captured German helmets. Another showed soldiers who had lost arms or legs in France. Their misfortune reminded me of Lon Justice, a twenty-year-old driver at Sprague Grocery, who was killed in Flanders. Dad had lettered a large sign in the Sprague warehouse, "Lon Justice—1900-1918—Gone But Not Forgotten."

Soon after the Victory Parade Mother and I moved out of Morningside Drive into a first floor apartment on West 104th Street. The apartment had an old-fashioned fireplace and a bay window opening on a tiny garden planted with violets. A bay window in the bedroom faced a small court where a slender aianthus tree struggled to reach the sunlight.

I spent some weeks getting used to the semi-slum environment of West 104th Street. It was a "play" street closed to traffic except for the Borden milk wagon with a horse that stopped from habit at the door of each customer. In afternoons the street was a bedlam of children playing baseball.

The neighborhood was composed of tradespeople and draftsmen who lived in a line of aging brownstone apartments. I came to like them. The manager of the Gristede grocery on Columbus Avenue gave me handfuls of peanuts. The hunchback selling *The New York Sunday*

Times under the El stairway saved the paper for me. I talked baseball with the blind old man who sold fresh horseradish on the sidewalk. There was Frank Giovanni who filled everybody's ice boxes since nobody could afford electric refrigerators. I offered to take Frank by subway out in the country, but he wouldn't leave 104th Street. "I'm scared," Frank said. "There's bad people out there."

An organ grinder and his monkey cruised 104th Street. If I dropped a nickel in the monkey's cup, he growled at me because I was so stingy. The street's one depressing spot was the building at the corner of 104th Street and Amsterdam Avenue. Its sign designated it as "A Home for Respectable, Aged and Indigent Females." In passing their dining room window, I watched them sitting, motionless and expressionless. They were just waiting to die I thought.

Before I started my fifth grade year at Horace Mann, Dad sent me my old bicycle—the one with the bent frame—for the ride to school. One day I left the bike at Gristede's and when I came out I watched a boy around the corner with my bike heading for Central Park. After that tragedy I roller-skated the mile up Broadway to Horace Mann.

One October afternoon friend Perry Driggs invited me to have dinner with him on Randall's Island in the East River where his father was superintendent of the reform school. From the 125th Street El station, Perry and I crossed to the East River dock to board the reform school's tug. We had a pleasant meal at the reform school.

Perry stayed at the reform school with his father. The tug returned me alone to 125th Street. I walked across 125th Street to the El Station. For whatever reason (except the carelessness of a ten-year-old) I climbed the El's uptown stairway instead of the downtown stairway. I put my last nickel in the gateway slot and boarded the uptown train. At 140th Street I noticed my mistake. I couldn't cross the El tracks to the downtown side. Because I had no nickel, the gateman would not let me through to the downtown train. There was nothing to do except to walk down Eighth Avenue from 140th Street through Harlem to West 104th Street. It was an eerie area in the dark. I was scared but I remembered the "Be Prepared" slogan of the Newark Boy Scout troop that I meant to join. I began walking south with my head held high, pretending that I was a First Class Boy Scout who had earned his hiking merit badge. Because of urgent need I slipped down a dark stairway to somebody's basement entry to relieve myself. Nobody shot a pistol at me in this delicate matter. I got home safely about midnight. Next day, Mother wrote a scathing letter to Mayor Hyland who replied that he would investigate the matter.

After Christmas of 1920 Mother was told by the principal of Horace Mann that I was to skip the fifth grade and go on to the sixth grade. My promotion prompted Mother to try to get a scholarship for me at a preparatory school in the fall of 1921. She knew that a Newark boy, Fleek Miller of the Hudson Avenue family, had attended Lawrenceville School near Trenton, New Jersey. She wrote the school's new headmaster, Mather Almon Abbott, about a scholarship for me.

Mother and I passed the winter of 1921 with the Lawrenceville scholarship matter up in the air. In mid-May when Horace Mann closed for the summer Dr. Abbott wrote Mother that I had been accepted for the First Form at Lawrenceville at a reduced all-expense tuition of $800 a year. Mother wrote Dad about Lawrenceville and Dad wrote back that he could afford the $800 tuition and that he was coming to New York to see us.

Dad drove from Newark to New York with his friend Fred Fenberg who owned Newark's Auditorium Theater. Fred was a tiny man and he had bought a twelve-cylinder Packard which was the "quality" car then like the Pierce Arrow and Peerless. The Packard was so huge that Fred could hardly see over the dashboard. The Packard went well over Uniontown Mountain, but when they reached Philadelphia Fred could not see the torn-up street ahead and went full speed into it tearing out the bottom of his Packard. Dad came on to New York by train.

At West 104th Street Mother told Dad that she was going to France with Damrosch school friends. To show his good will Dad agreed to pay for her passage on the Veendam. Then he took the three of us on a ride up the Hudson River Day Line past West Point. It was a nice ride on a beautiful stretch of the Hudson. But on the return downstream Mother and Dad got into a heated argument. I did not get the details of it, but I think Mother asked Dad to cooperate if she sued him for a divorce so that she could marry Charlie Drake. The distress of arguing gave Mother a headache. When the boat stopped at Yonkers she stepped on the boat dock to buy aspirin for a headache. Suddenly without warning the boat moved off without Mother. As Dad and I watched from the deck, Mother rushed up waving her empty pocket book at us. Several hours later we found her at home, worn out by the hot Broadway trolley ride all the way from Yonkers down to 104th Street. We put her to bed and administered hot tea.

Chapter Four

MARCHING FOR LAWRENCE

— 1926 —

AFTER OUR Hudson Day line adventure, Mother, Dad and I took the 23rd Street ferry to Hoboken to see Mother off to Europe on the Veendam. Then Dad and I rode the Pennsy train to Newark. I was looking forward to joining the Newark Boy Scouts. The scout camp was on a farm near Mount Vernon. Dad persuaded his small friend, Fred Fenberg, to take me and a carload of boys to the scout camp in his repaired Packard. On Horn's Hill Fred drove around a curve too fast and slid his big car into a farmer's barbed wire fence doing still more damage to his Packard.

Scouting went well. I took pride in becoming a First Class Scout at the camp at age twelve. That status allowed me to wear the uniform, especially the Boy Scout hat which I thought made me look bigger and more handsome.

In September of 1921 I rode to Trenton where Mother met me and took me in a taxi five miles north toward Princeton to start my First Form at Lawrenceville. I knew nothing about the place and it was not until years later that I learned the history of the school from S. R. Slaymaker II's excellent book *Five Miles Away*. Lawrenceville was not a newcomer in the prep school field. The first private school in America was Phillips Academy, Andover, Massachusetts (1778) followed by Phillips Exeter Academy, Exeter, New Hampshire (1781). Lawrenceville began in 1810 in New Jersey with nine students as "The Academy of Maidenhead." Fortunately, it was renamed "Lawrenceville" in

1816. These early private schools were created to meet the needs of universities like Harvard (1636), Yale (1701) and Princeton (1746), for students who were better prepared, thus the term "preparatory" schools.

Lawrenceville's growth was slow until 1875 when John Cleve Green, who had attended the school in 1810, willed it part of his large fortune. Rapid growth followed with the building by 1896 of the five "Circle Houses"—roughly Boston-Romanesque or Tudor in style. The circular campus was designed by Frederick Olmstead who had created Central Park in New York. All the five Circle Houses are in service today.

An unexpected factor in Lawrenceville's growth after 1900 was the graduation in 1895 of a sixteen-year-old New York City boy named Owen McMahon Johnson. This boy had sold a story for one dollar to *St. Nicholas Magazine* when he was six years old. In his first year at Lawrenceville he founded a magazine written by the students which today is called *The Lit*. In 1908 Owen Johnson wrote *The Prodigious Hickey* the first of his two novels based on his experiences at Lawrenceville. The popularity of these books put the school on the map. One *New York Times* book reviewer called Johnson "the Homer of the American Prep school." Another reviewer judged Johnson's book *The Varmint* to be "pretty close to Tarkington's *Seventeen*" and *Tom Brown's School Days*." Before World War I boys who had read *The Prodigious Hickey* wanted to go to Lawrenceville, not for education but to find out if the scoops of ice cream at the Jigger Shop were as tasty as the book's Egghead and Gutter Pup said they were. Perhaps some boys got indigestion emulating Hungry Smeed's record consumption of forty-nine pancakes in an hour.

The prodigious Hickey's craftiness was shown on prime time TV as recently as 1988 when all of Owen Johnson's Lawrenceville books were republished.

Mother's taxi took the two of us to Rosehill House where she turned me over to Mr. Cole, the house master, and left me to return to New York. Rosehill was one of ten detached houses for first formers. This "small house system" was patterned on a similar plan at Eton.

Rosehill was an independent unit with its own cook. Each small house had its own football and baseball team (if short of players Mr. Cole played) competing with the other small houses. The houses competed scholastically, too.

At my first Rosehill dinner I met the other nine boys, aged twelve to fifteen. Most of them came from the vicinity of New York City. One of them from Philadelphia was Chester Pond who proclaimed that he weighed seventy pounds and was the smallest boy at Lawrenceville. (I weighed seventy-three pounds.) The boys nicknamed Chester Pond "Hercules." Later on they nicknamed me "Goop Ears."

I had become used to New York City boys at Horace Mann. Mother had strained her budget to dress me properly. One of the boys from Long Island wore knickers from Brooks Brothers and saddle shoes from Frank Brothers. I thought my clothes were as stylish as theirs because I was a card-bearing Third Degree Ropeco which meant that Mother had bought for me enough clothes from Rogers Peet Company to achieve ROPECO status.

It took me a few weeks to learn the ropes at Lawrenceville. Chester Pond and I rode Chester's bicycle tandem along the golf course to the Circle and Dr. Abbott's Foundation House and on to Edith Memorial Chapel for the compulsory morning prayer to get our studies off with God's help. Historically, Lawrenceville was Presbyterian but it had enough Episcopalian ritual to please both kinds of parents. Moving along the seven-hole golf course with Hercules and me were the students of Davis House near Rosehill—a large off-Circle House. The assistant master of Davis House, a slender young man wearing cockleshell glasses often trotted along beside our tandem bicycles. Mr. Cole told us that his name was Thornton Wilder and that he had come to Lawrenceville from Rome in August to teach French.

Of course, I was homesick now and then that first year. I didn't mind the Rosehill House hazing of the "rhinies"—making us walk after dark among the graves of the Presbyterian cemetery. But I hated having to get out of my warm bed at 6 A.M. on sub-zero nights to close the windows of the "old" boys. I enjoyed the Thanksgiving dinner at Rosehill when Mr. Cole passed out cigars and I got sick trying to smoke them. In the fall we played cops and robbers in the big meadow behind Phillips House. Once during a cloud burst we decided to ignore the rain by playing touch football in the Rosehill yard. The idea was to see which of us could get the most mud on our feet, clothes and face.

My biggest trial that first year was adjusting myself to Dr. Abbott's system of punishment for delinquency and misconduct. I had never been disciplined—not by my loving parents or by the teachers at Horace Mann. Dr. Abbott's mark system punished boys with two marks for missing a class, four marks for misconduct in class, and worst of all, five marks for whatever evil act "Bott" Abbott thought a boy committed. Boys who accumulated sixty-four marks were expelled.

A boy had to "walk off" or "sit off" all his marks before he could leave school for his Christmas vacation. It took two hours sitting alone in the boy's room to expunge eight marks. A boy could expunge only twenty-four marks in one day of sitting. If he had twenty-four marks he had to lose a whole day of his Christmas vacation. This mark system cost me two or three vacation days. But I certainly needed the Bott's discipline and I "walked off" my marks in a constructive way. Sitting in my room I learned to juggle tennis balls and to blow smoke rings.

I wasted no time that fall getting to Owen Johnson's Jigger Shop to try the Prodigious Hickey's ice cream scoops. I also ate hundreds of "bracers' which were Hershey bars between buttered toast.

Of all Lawrenceville's buildings, I liked best the stately gymnasium. Inside the gym was the basketball court lined with bars and weight-lifting rigs. An iron circular staircase led up to the padded running track which circled the gym—twenty-one laps to a mile. The twenty-five yard swimming pool was in the basement near the rifle range. Because of my long-distance swimming with Dad at Buckeye Lake I was the best of First Form swimmers. My specialty was swimming under water.

Exercise classes were compulsory at Lawrenceville. They were conducted by a bespectacled man named Lory Prentiss. He was at least seventy years old, but he could do a back flip from a standing start without even taking off his glasses.

The Rosehill boys enjoyed poking fun at me as a boy from a town in Ohio that they had never heard of. I bolstered my self-esteem by wearing my handsome Boy Scout hat to classes. I began to sense that the boys did not think much of my hat when they had a meeting and voted to forbid me to wear my Boy Scout hat on the grounds that it was a silly hat.

I was unhappy about their view because I did not have the money to buy their style of hat. But I thought of a way to solve the problem. I had seen a sleek Brooks Brothers hat hanging unclaimed in the Mem Hall cloak room. It fit me, so I borrowed it. One day in the Jigger Shop I felt myself being spun around by somebody. It was Jack Sickel, a star on the track team. He said, "So you are the louse who stole my hat." He yanked it off my head. He said, "You ought to know, Rhinie, that we don't allow thieves at Lawrenceville. Your case is one for the Discipline Committee. Be in my room in Upper House on Sunday."

I recall no time in my life as painful as that day when I walked to Jack Sickel's room with two stern members of the Discipline Committee standing by. Jack stood waving a coat hanger at me which I thought he planned to beat me with. He talked at length about the evils of theft. Finally, he said, "Well, Sprague" we'll let you go this time. But don't let it happen again." I said, "Yes, sir!" and ran out of Upper House skyborn with relief.

Because of their displeasure with my Boy Scout hat, the Rosehill boys were standoffish with me. But before I left for Christmas vacation with Mother in New York, it was announced that I had won the First Form Poetry prize. The prize was *An American Anthology.* My poetry prize gave Rosehill enough merit points to lead all the small houses. Thereafter the Rosehill boys treated me with some respect.

———

For my Third and Fourth Form years at Lawrenceville, I moved from Rosehill to Hamill House near the Circle. Dad had given me a crankup Victrola so that I could listen to the Mound City Blue Blowers and Ukulele Ike. I was a poor student at Lawrenceville—too many distractions. In February there was the Midwinter Prom. Dad bought me a tuxedo for it. Nothing in my later life compared with the excitement of those three Prom days. I wrote a poem for the Prom Edition of *The Lit*—"The Promme" (With Apologies to Chaucer, G)—

> 'Twas in the wintere tyme of this leape yere,
> When damsels did theire new Roulles Roucyes stire
> Upon an pilgrimage to Lawrencetoune,
> All semely dressed in sheekish hat and gonne.
> The place, wherewith was held this blessed hoppe,
> Where all the faere maidens therewith did stoppe,
> Was a most beauteous gyme a mar'vlous sight,
> Among the ladies was a beauteous gyrle
> Wythe louvely cheeks and yes like the pearle.
> And faere rounde armes and pretty armes in pout—
> Methinks this gyrle was what is called an knock
> owet!
> There was alsoe wythe them a chaperone,

Methinks that she was maede of bonne,
Who couldley turned her crooked upturned snoute
Wyth scorne towards maides a-smoking cigaroutte.
Prommes are I very truly must confess
By farr moure joyous than words ex-presse.

M.S.

The Prom frenzy began on Friday when the Lawrence, the school paper, published the names of the girls who were attending. They came from all the famous eastern girl's schools, from Ogontz and Dana Hall, Rosemary, Madeira, Briarcliffe, Bennett, Sweetbriar and West-over. The Prom Committee hired Tantum's in Trenton to drape the gym in tons of bunting, giving it the effect of an oriental bordello. The best dance bands in the land were hired. I remember Zez Confrey's band played with Zez himself playing "Kitten on the Keys" and "Stumbling." Bott Abbott stopped Confrey's music for half an hour, saying that the music stimulated "risque dancing."

Everybody danced the Charleston. I can still see those hundreds of girls flinging out their legs with piston-like precision. I cut in on smaller girls, leaving the tall gorgeous Prom trotters like Kitty North, Bobby Baxter and Charlotte Skoonmaker to star athletes. All of us tried to entice a girl up the gym's staircase to the nooks near the running track where we could hold her hand out of the view of the faculty chaperons.

After the Prom I was inspired by Zez Confrey's jazz piano to study the stride piano as played by a tall lanky Bill Candy from St. Louis. Bill had the big hands required for 'stride' piano because he could stretch with his left hand from C to E. Bill played in the gym at the Saturday night movies. He spiced up the movie with renditions of "Hard Hearted Hannah, the Vamp of Savannah."

I asked Bill Candy how I could learn to play jazz. He said, "Get a chord book. There are only three chords in most tunes."

For my remaining years at Lawrenceville I drove everybody crazy practicing chord progressions. The 1926 Olla Pod year book wrote about me: "Whoever has heard the Upper House crash with melodious discords and above the din heard a voice chanting 'Dinah' in reckless abandon can be sure Marsh is at work removing the pent-up exuberance of his soul."

I spent Spring vacation with Mother in New York. Dad wrote me that Uncle Hal's wife, my Aunt Rose, had died in London. He was bringing her body to Newark for burial in the Sprague lot. Dad said Aunt Rose had left shares of Sprague Meter stock to a dozen of her Sprague relatives as she had no children. I was very sad about Aunt Rosie's death. She had always been good to me. She had taken me in New York to see "The Miracle" which had starred Lady Diana Manners as the Madonna and Roseamond Pinchot as the nun. I wrote an ecstatic review of it for *The Lit*.

My review of "The Miracle" reminded me that I intended to be a writer. Accordingly, I wrote a story for *The Lit* titled "The Broker" about a Wall Street crook. For realism I borrowed the name of a real Wall Street broker, the father of one of my classmates. My crook story did not please the father, who complained about the story to Dr. Abbott. I got five black marks for my first published story.

Even so I was elected to *The Lit* board of editors just before Thornton Wilder became *The Lit's* faculty supervisor. This was done because Mr. Wilder had written a novel called *The Cabala*. He was said to be planning a second novel about Peru.

———

I rode the Pennsy to Newark for summer vacation. At the station, Dad told me that Uncle Hal wanted to send me to Valley Ranch in Wyoming on an eight-week horseback ride through Yellowstone Park. Dad said that Uncle Hal could afford the cost of the trip because his Sprague Meter Company had prospered. I had always been fond of Uncle Hal because he had always kept an eye on the welfare of his relatives in Newark.

In July I boarded in Chicago the Valley Ranch special car with the forty-five boys who were making the horseback trip. In Cody, Wyoming, I was assigned a small pony (I named him George). Uncle Hal had given me money to buy my cowboy outfit—chaps, spurs, neckerchief and a Stetson hat bigger than my old Boy Scout hat.

We rode our horses twenty-five miles on our first day out of Cody up Shoshone Canyon and on to Old Faithful. For eight weeks we tenderfoot cowboys roamed the back trails of that beautiful park. The trip ended with a party at Jackson Lake below the Tetons with the Valley Ranch girl riders.

Back home in Newark I refused to take off any part of my cowboy outfit. I spent days striding around the Newark Square bowlegged in my Stetson hat and chaps with my spurs tinkling and a Lucky Strike drooping in my mouth. To Dad's amusement I insisted on sleeping outdoors in the back yard until the ants and rain forced me to give up being a cowboy and move indoors.

Back at Lawrenceville in September of 1925 for my Fifth Form year, I reviewed the ups and downs of my four high school years. I had failed to win the Fourth Form Declamation Contest. I suffered an even greater humiliation a year later. I had a date to meet a girl in New York under the clock of the Biltmore Hotel and take her tea dancing at 10 East 60th Street where Rudy Vallee was the big attraction. For the occasion I thought it proper to wear a raccoon coat which I borrowed from a classmate. My date did not show up under the Biltmore clock, so I went on alone to 10 East 60th Street (Villa Venice). I took a table near Rudy Vallee's band and listened to Rudy crooning "I'm Just a Vagabond Lover." I drank several cups of tea and languidly smoked a pack of cigarettes. After an hour or so I left Villa Venice and hailed a taxi. As I stepped into the cab the heat of the raccoon cot and the smoking overcame me and I upchucked gallons of tea all over the inside of the cab. I gave the cab driver five dollars to clean up the mess.

On the whole, I realized that Lawrenceville had been good for me. I had learned how to get to classes on time, how to dance the Charleston, and how to play jazz piano. My masters had taught me how to study—that knowing something was a lot more fun than not knowing. Most of the masters were dedicated men. Thornton Wilder was my favorite. All of us in his French class found him to be immensely appealing in his eagerness to push his knowledge of the French subjunctive into our cluttered heads. He was in his twenties with a frame on the lean and hungry side. He had a quick smile and probing eyes that seemed to find us as intriguing as monkeys in the zoo. We were delighted when our conduct threw him into a fit of anger. He calmed himself by hurling erasers at us and cursing us in colloquial French.

As the *Lit* faculty supervisor, Mr. Wilder encouraged us to write as we pleased. He urged us to study the style of contemporary writers such as Warner Fabian's *Flaming Youth* and Homer Croy's tragic tale of an unmarried girl's pregnancy in a small town. I waded through John Galsworthy's *The Forsythe Saga.*

It is not easy to write believably about Mather A. Abbott. For fifteen years until his death in 1934 he was the most colorful of prep school headmasters. At age forty-five, he was rather short and stocky with an oversized head. His shoulders were a yard wide and he had the deep chest of a Hereford bull. His characteristic stance was like that of a bull pawing the earth and ready to charge anything in his way.

He had a pathological belief in the correctness of his judgment. Anybody who opposed him could expect to be locked in the stockade with a dunce cap on his head. He was anathema to many students, masters, alumni, trustees and donors to endowment funds. He was as tyrannical as Louis XIV, Napoleon and the Kaiser Wilhelm. But when he was angry, nobody dared oppose him for fear of being gored.

Dr. Abbott was born in Nova Scotia in 1874 of an English family. He grew up in England and attended Worcester College where he was a top athlete in football, cricket and crew. He taught Latin for twenty years at Groton where Franklin D. Roosevelt was a student. He taught at Yale and served there during World War I in a U.S. training unit.

I became used to his triumphant cry, "Five black marks!" Among the black marks the Bott gave me, I remember best the ones he gave me at Prom time to discourage sex and misbehavior. He had ruled that nobody could leave the Esplanade of Upper House with their girls. My date at that Prom was with a girl whose father was an architect. She asked me to see the new Father's Building to tell her father about it. As we returned to the Esplanade the Bott rushed up to me and my girl. "Sprague," he shouted, "what have you been doing?" I said, "I have been showing my date the Father's Building, Sir!" "That's a lie!" the Bott said. "Five black marks!"

Next day the Bott wrote Dad that I was a liar and not likely to graduate. I wrote Dad the facts and told him my grades were in good shape. Of course, I forgave Bott in the end. I even admitted that he and his black marks had done a great deal for me to improve the handling of my affairs. At commencement in June 1926, as I stepped up in white flannels for my diploma, the Bott handed me my diploma, gave me a half smile, patted me on my head, and murmured, "Good boy."

Chapter Five

TRUCKING FOR DAD

I SAW VERY little of my sister Josie during my five years away from Newark at Lawrenceville. I was glad to catch up with her when she came to my graduation with her new husband Howie Taylor (of the South Dakota Taylors, not the Newark Taylors).

Josie married Howie in 1924 after she made a world cruise with Uncle Hal who was desperately unhappy after Aunt Rosie's death. To take his mind off her death, he took Josie out of school and brought her with him to his Moana Hotel in Honolulu where they boarded the White Star liner Belgenland for its cruise around the world. From the ship at Calcutta, Josie rode the train to Agra to see the Taj Mahal. Reaching Cairo, she posed for a photo sitting on top of a camel. She slipped off the camel, breaking a front tooth.

On the Belgenland several passengers looking for husbands succumbed to Uncle Hal's elusive charm. His most ardent admirer was the Princess of Braganza, a member by marriage of Portugal's royal family, though this princess was born in Cincinnati, Ohio, not Portugal.

To chaperon Josie on the Belgenland, Uncle Hal brought along a lady from Stuttgart, Germany. The chaperon told Josie that she was getting along in years (Josie was twenty-two), and she should be finding a husband. She said she had one in mind for Josie, a handsome bachelor named Howard Taylor who was a consul in the Stuttgart American Consulate. She arranged for Howard to meet Josie in Paris when her cruise ended there.

Howie came to Paris and fell in love with Josie. They were married by the Justice de Paix in Montmartre. Attendants at the wedding were Uncle Hal as best man for Josie, the Princess of Braganza as maid of honor, and by chance, William Phelps Eno, Uncle Hal's roommate at Yale in 1881. Eno, a traffic expert, was in Paris supervising the installation of one-way streets as he had in New York and London.

———

In June when Josie and Howie left me after my graduation, I boarded the Pennsy in Trenton bound for Newark. My express did not stop in Newark that week, but Dad and I knew that it had to make a safety stop at East Main street short of the Newark depot near Pete the Greek's cafe. When my train stopped, I leaped from the vestibule to the rubble by the track without breaking my ankle. The porter tossed me my suitcase.

I found Dad waiting for me at Pete the Greek's. Dad was sixty-six then but looked older. As always he listened intently to my report of what Mother was doing in New York. I knew that he still loved her and was always ready to help her even after her marriage in 1922 to Charlie Drake. That marriage had ended in an amicable divorce because Charlie was away from New York most of the time managing the concerts of the virtuoso Jascha Heifitz.

I told Dad that Mother had changed her name to "Grace" from "Della" because she thought "Grace" had a more polished sound to it. She had given up her ambition to be a concert pianist and had shipped her Steinway to Josie in Stuttgart. She had turned her creative impulse to writing a novel about Newark. Recently, she had persuaded the editor of *Women's Wear Daily* to send her to Paris to report on what fashionable ladies were wearing in resorts like Biarritz and Monte Carlo. Dad smiled at my mention of Mother's sudden entry into journalism. "That's Della all over," Dad said. "Your Mother is a remarkable woman, Marshall. Look at all she has done for you."

As Dad and I left Pete the Greek's, Dad told me that he had a summer job for me at $20 a week driving the Sprague's Model-T truck delivering groceries to outlying villages like Toboso and Hanover. There are few thrills in life like one's first paying job. After breakfast I would stroll to work down our alley, a languid Lucky Strike in my mouth, aglow with self-esteem.

At the Sprague warehouse, I would crank the Model-T engine half-a-turn so as not to break my arm if the engine backfired. My Model-T had three drive pedals—forward, reverse and brake. If the brakes failed, the truck could be stopped by pushing the reverse pedal.

All three Sprague's warehouse men were kind to me that summer, although my teen-age miscues must have pained them. They warned me not to overload the ancient elevator that served the third floor, so, of course, I piled it high with cases. When I stepped on it, my weight caused the elevator to make a dignified descent past the main floor to the basement.

In 1926, my idol was the muscle-man Charles Atlas. One of my truck loads included a five hundred gallon barrel of vinegar to deliver to a grocery in Toboso. Being Charles Atlas, I eased the barrel to the edge of the truck and let it bump its way down off the truck to the ground. I rolled it into the grocery and returned to Newark. When I got there, I found Dad talking on the phone. "Do you mean to tell me," he said, "that son of mine brought you a barrel of vinegar, and it sprung a leak, and your store is an inch deep in vinegar?"

Ever since Mother left Dad in 1920, I worried about its effect on his well-being, but I could see as I worked with him that summer that he managed to get some pleasure out of life. He enjoyed his job as buyer for the grocery. His drummers liked to tell him embroidered tales of their amorous adventures and misadventures—with ladies in Pullman cars and in cities all over Ohio. As Dad talked with the drummers, he made pencil sketches of their faces. His sketches delighted the drummers who had them framed and took them home to their wives.

I think that Dad's happiest hours were spent when he retired to his leather couch in his bedroom to read the latest copy of *The Saturday Evening Post*. The 1920s were great years for the *Post* under the editorship of George Horace Larimer. Dad read everything in the *Post* from Edith Wharton to the Miami gambling stories of Joseph Hergesheimer and Booth Tarkington's yarns about the Terrible Tempered Mr. Bang. He read the Earthworm Tractor and Tugboat Annie stories. I would hear him roaring with laughter over the escapades of Florian Slappey in Birmingham.

———

In July, Uncle Hal came to Newark and invited Dad and Aunt Mary to spend a fortnight with him in Honolulu at the Moana Hotel. As a kindly gesture, he took along Anna Glover, the widowed sister of

Uncle George's late wife. Dad told me that Anna Glover was delighted to be invited hoping that Uncle Hal planned to marry her during the trip as an antidote for his loneliness.

Uncle Hal did not marry Anna Glover. He did not return to Newark when his Honolulu guests came home. Dad explained to me that Uncle Hal had not felt well in Honolulu. His doctor diagnosed his heart pains as angina. He assigned to Uncle Hal a beautiful thirty-year-old nurse named Helen Magnus, who specialized in the care of heart patients. When Uncle Hal, aged seventy-two, left Honolulu he took Helen Magnus along with him. He married her on their arrival at Uncle Hal's house in Black Rock near Bridgeport.

In spite of the age difference, it turned out to be a happy marriage lasting until Uncle Hal's death at age eighty in 1937. In 1931, my "Aunt" Helen presented Uncle Hal with a son—Henry Hezekiah Sprague II. At the fiftieth reunion of Uncle Hal's Class of 1881 at Yale he was given a handsome silver cup engraved "in Honor of the Last Class Baby 1881."

———

In mid-August, word came to me in Newark from Dean Heermance, Princeton's flamboyant dean of admissions, that I had been admitted to Princeton Class of 1930. To please Uncle Hal I had applied for entrance to both Princeton and Yale, but I preferred Princeton because the name had a more romantic ring to it. Also, people always said that Princeton was more like a country club than a college. Since Lawrenceville graduates went to Princeton, going there was almost like returning to Lawrenceville.

I worried a little because I did not know where I would live in Princeton. Freshmen rarely were assigned rooms on campus unless they were the sons of alumni. My room problem was solved when my old friends, the identical twins, Allen and Chick Shenk, invited me to share the cost of three rooms they had leased at 66 Nassau Street above Louis Kaplan's clothing store and Skirm's Smoke Shop.

I wondered how dad would feel about the extra expense of Princeton. Dad had told me that the Sprague Grocery would have to close soon because the Kroger chain stores were coming to Newark. But Dad said not to worry—because he was making money for a change. He had sold his Buckeye Lake farm with its mile of lake front to a

Columbus realtor who had transformed it with roads and utilities into a popular Columbus resort called Harbor Hills. Dad and the realtor split fifty-fifty the sale of the farm's hundreds of high-priced lots.

Aunt Mary sewed name tapes on my clothes as I prepared to enter Princeton in September. It made me sad to leave my friends at the Sprague grocery. They had given me a happy summer. The trucking job took so much of my energy that I was ready for bed after supper. I read a lot of best-selling books in bed such as Warner Fabian's *Flaming Youth,* which described the scandalous behavior of Josie's generation during the "Roaring Twenties." I wept over Homer Crory's tragic story *West of the Water Tower* about an unmarried girl in a small town who was driven to suicide by the mean-spirited gossip of her neighbors over her pregnancy.

I marvelled at the beauty of F. Scott Fitzgerald's prose in *All the Sad Young Men* and wondered how this brilliant Princetonian had been able to write so well as a teen-ager. I lapped up Richard Halliburton's adventure book *The Royal Road to Romance.* I hoped that some day I could be like Halliburton by swimming the Hellespont, sleeping in the Taj Mahal, and "spitting a mile" from the top of the Matterhorn. I still dreamed of becoming a writer. I spent one Sunday writing the first act of a play in the irreverent style of George Bernard Shaw. My play, I decided, was better than Shaw's whose people talked too much and did not get around to doing anything interesting.

Chapter Six

"Tourist Third"

IN SEPTEMBER I spent $140 that I had saved from my job as a truck driver. I bought my share of furniture from the Student Exchange for our rooms at 66 Nassau Street where some previous student had left a battered upright piano. Our rooms faced the cement posts and iron grill of the main gate leading to Nassau Hall. The rooms were near Holder Court and the freshman dining halls. They were close to the "Balt" restaurant where upper classmen with hangovers bought coffee and ham and eggs at outrageous prices.

I had decided to major in English. I still dreamed of becoming a writer some day, but I did not want to try out for the *Daily Princetonian* or the *Nassau Literary Magazine.* I had worn out my interest in school publications at Lawrenceville.

While I was trying to decide what to do with myself at Princeton, the matter was decided for me by the sort of accident that shapes everybody's lives. A freshman from Chicago named Jack Howe had the rooms above ours. We often heard Jack practicing on his tenor saxophone. Jack was a handsome man not much larger than his sax. He talked with explosive enthusiasm about jazz and the musical revolution in Chicago caused by the kind of improvised jazz played by King Oliver and his musicians from New Orleans.

Jack said that he had played in the Chicago Latin School band with his best friend Jimmy McPartland who was later married to the English jazz pianist Marian McPartland. The Latin School band's big rival was the Austin High School Band. It featured a sixteen-year-old clarinet player named Benny Goodman and other young musicians like Bud Freeman and Dave Tough who would win national jazz celebrity.

To improve their technique, Jack Howe and Jimmy McPartland spent the summer of 1926 following the one-night stands of the Wolverine dance band. The members of that band included a twenty-three-year-old cornet player named Bix Beiderbecke and a soprano sax man, Frankie Trumbauer. The band's arranger was Hoagy Carmichael who wrote jam tunes for the Wolverines like "Riverboat Shuffle." Carmichael was inspired by the melodic quality of Beiderbeck's solos to write a song he called "Stardust" which would become one of the most enduring of all popular songs.

At Jack's urging I bought an 1926 recording of the Wolverine Band. The two of us listened in bemused admiration to Beiderbecke's cornet solo of "Singin' the Blues" on that record. Trumpeters to this day play it note for note. It made Beiderbecke a jazz legend long after his death of alcoholism in 1931 at age twenty-eight. The beauty of his phrasing and timing remains without equal.

One day I was plunking out the Princeton anthem "Tiger Rag" on the upright. Jack Howe came in and watched me playing. When I stopped, Jack said, "Those are the wrong chords. Let me show you the right ones." He sat down at the piano and played several strange chords. I learned them later—augmented and diminished ninths and elevenths. After his piano lesson, Jack said, "I am starting a band to play twice a week for dinners in Freshman Commons. The college will pay the band $60 a week. I want you to play the piano in my band." I said that I didn't play well enough for that. Jack said "Never mind—you have a good beat." "Jack" I said, "It's a metronome beat I learned from beating my feet to my mother's metronome as she played Chopin." Jack said, "Well, I'd rather have a good beat than a good pianist! We'll call the band the Black Cap Six." (Freshmen at Princeton had to wear little black beanies called "dinks" to mark their lowly status.)

In mid-October, the Black Cap Six began playing at dinner in Freshman Commons. Jack's was the usual Dixieland combo—trumpet, sax, drums, string bass and piano. None of us, except Jack, could read music. We improvised the tune by ear and knew the rudiments of harmony. I played the right piano chords because Jack called them out to me—G7, D7, A7, E7, in the standard jazz progression. Jack gave us the key for a song with raised fingers. One finger was the key of F, two fingers was Bb, three fingers was Eb.

Our music at the Commons was ragged, but the freshmen loved it. We played the popular tunes of 1926—"My Cutie's Due at Two, Two, Two," "Tea for Two," "Sometimes I'm Happy," "Hallelujah." When we played "I Wanna Be Loved by You," the Commons rocked as the freshmen roared out "Boop-boop-a-doop" imitating Helen Kane's squeaky singing. We played "Cross Your Heart" because in 1926 the freshmen were in love with Mary Lawlor, the star of the musical "Ocean High."

I should mention that those first months of our freshman year were a wobbly period for both the Shenk twins and for me. The trouble was that we could not adjust to the freedom of life at Princeton after the years all of us had spent under the discipline that Dr. Abbott imposed upon us at Lawrenceville—no smoking, no gambling, no drinking, no vulgar language, no girls. At Princeton, we played black jack and poker until dawn every Saturday night. For liquor, Prohibition forced us to drink a kind of pink syrup needled with homemade grain alcohol. We drank it—a lot of it.

The Shenks had edited the yearbook at Lawrenceville. They had placed apt quotes under the photos of each graduate. The quote under my photo read "I am bad, I am wicked, but I hope to be worse after a while." The quote was by an eighteenth-century minister, Thomas Binney.

It was easy to be bad at Princeton. But some freshmen pushed their badness beyond the limits of normal student misbehavior. I remember a freshman who picked up a hooker in Philadelphia and installed her near Carmine George's speakeasy far out on Witherspoon Street. Having learned that New Jersey police would not bother her unless she contributed to the delinquency of a minor, the hooker accepted the business of Princeton seniors only. A week passed before the Princeton proctors Frank and Harry persuaded her to move her business to Trenton.

A freshman friend of mine decided to make Princeton history by bringing a hooker to sophomore prom. He found her at the corner of Lexington and 42nd Street and installed her for the weekend at Nassau Inn, assuring the manager that his prom date was a freshman at Vassar majoring in social science. The girl enjoyed great popularity at the prom.

When I tried to be bad, it always seemed to rebound. For instance, one day that fall I went, bound for fun and frolic, to a Princeton-Yale football game and dance at New Haven. At six the next morning a cop woke me up. I was still in my tux, having missed my train and spent the night on the hard bench in the New Haven Railroad Station.

I would learn during my Christmas vacation that to be bad could be costly. After my mother had divorced Charlie Drake, I saw him now and then. Of course, he knew of my interest in George Gershwin's music so he took me with him to a Christmas party that Jascha Heifetz was giving. The party was in the apartment on Central Park West of Heifetz's father-in-law, Samuel Chotzinoff. It was a very large party of elegant people, including many prominent musicians. What impressed me the most, however, was quite a large bar operated by a professional bartender. He was serving Scotch whisky which, he told me, was delivered that day from Montreal. After the nauseating liquor I had been drinking at Princeton, I lapped up this delightful Scotch even faster than did the other guests. It wasn't long before I found that I wasn't very steady on my feet. As I wobbled along, a stern young man wearing a large sombrero walked up to me. It was Jascha Heifetz. He said to me, "I don't believe I know you." With a jaunty wave of the hand, I replied, "Well, I don't know you either." Heifetz walked on. Two minutes later Charlie Drake took me by the arm. "I'm sending you home, Marsh. You're drunk." It was about ten o'clock. He put me in a taxi and sent me to his hotel. I learned from Charlie Drake later that no sooner had I left the Heifetz party than George Gershwin, who was a marvelous pianist, arrived. He loved to entertain at parties. He sat down at the piano and played until 3 A.M. He had just written the music for "Tiptoes" with his brother Ira. "Tiptoes" had some of the tunes and lyrics I loved best. Gershwin must have played all of them that night—"Looking for a Boy," "That Certain Feeling," "Clap Yo Hands," "Lady, Be Good." For the rest of my life I have regretted deeply having missed those hours of music by one of the greatest composers and jazz pianists of all time.

George Gershwin died in California of a brain tumor in 1937, aged thirty-eight. I mourned his death and am eternally grateful for the joy his music gave and still gives me.

———

I was so unhappy about missing an evening with George Gerswhin that I decided to greatly reduce my drinking. I did make a few visits with the Shenks to Honest Abe's Saloon at the end of the interurban street-car line from Princeton to Trenton.

Abe was a nice man, but he banned freshmen from his saloon because one of us busted a window on his slot machines so that we could stick a finger in and stop the whirling three cherries at their pay off line. We paid for our dinner with the pay-off quarters until Abe got suspicious and discovered the broken window of his slot machine. That ended our welcome at Abe's Saloon in Trenton.

Meanwhile the Black Cap Six earned a little money playing for faculty parties and for the monthly dances of Miss Fine's School for Girls. Occasionally Jack Howe and I went to New York for a weekend at night clubs and speakeasies. First, we went to the Clam and Broth House in Hoboken and crossed to New York on the 21st Street Ferry. Next we stopped at Frank and Giletti's brownstone on West 46th Street. It was a sedate place like almost all the New York speakeasies, requiring coat and tie for entry and no boisterous behavior. Then, we would stop at Leon and Eddie's and Brazaratti's on 46th street and at Julius' big saloon at 10th and Waverly Street in Greenwich Village. Julius' saloon was famous for its free lunch of assorted cheeses. It had never been closed during the dry thirteen years of Prohibition. We were told that it was protected by Tammany Hall.

After the Village, we would go up to Roseland, a ten-cents-a-dance hall, to hear Fletcher Henderson's band. We listened to Duke Ellington's band at the Cotton Club in Harlem. We would stop at Connie's Inn where Louis Armstrong was beginning a fabulous career as a world-renowned trumpet player. We would wind up at Moriarty's Speakeasy on 58th Street. Dan Moriarty's was a favorite of the Yale men because it was near Grand Central Station where they could catch the last "Owl" trains to New Haven. Jack and I would spend the night at the Princeton Club at Park Avenue and 41st Street.

In April 1927 Jack Howe called his band to 66 Nassau Street. A man from the Cunard Steamship Line was lining up bands to play dance music for the Tourist Third sailings on Cunard ships. Most of the steamship companies had discovered in the 1920s a way to use their unprofitable steerage space. They put in dining rooms, bar rooms, shuffleboards and two bunk cabins in layers three decks below. They offered college students Tourist Third trips from New York to France for $150 round trip. Companies found that the students liked the slow ten-day crossings. To do this, Tourist Third ships ran at half speed. The savings in fuel more than met the cost of feeding the students during the extra days at sea.

As Jack Howe was setting us up to audition, the Cunard agent said, "Never mind the audition. I know you play well enough. Can you be in New York at Cunard's 14th Street dock on June 16? You will play to France for Tourist Third on our *S. S. Tuscania.* We will give the band the round trip free for your music." The Cunard man said that he would call our band the "Tiger Cubs" in advertising to show that we were from Princeton. The *Tuscania* would bring the band back from France to New York early in August.

Jack and I spent spring vacation at 66 Nassau Street getting our music ready for "Tourist Third." We stole tunes from the Brunswick records of a new band, "Red Nichols and His Five Pennies."

Ted Wells, a sophomore friend of mine from Wichita, Kansas, came by one day to watch us copying the Nichols records. Ted asked me if I would like to fly in his Jenny biplane for a round of golf on the Lawrenceville golf course. I had never gone up in a plane, so I was glad to accept Ted's offer. I knew that Ted's father worked for Beech Aircraft and that Ted had been flying since he was twelve years old. He had bought his old Jenny plane from Army surplus for $700. He kept it in a field out on Prospect Street.

I climbed into the open cockpit of the Jenny while Ted spun the propeller by hand and leaped into his cockpit when the engine started. In the air the engine sputtered a little but somehow we arrived safely at the Lawrenceville golf course. We landed on the fairway near Dawes House and the tee of the fourth hole, which ran four hundred yards or so to the trees and telephone lines along Lincoln Highway. Ted left me to get gasoline for the thirty-mile flight to New Brunswick to have the Jenny's oil changed. To correct the engine's sputter, Ted said that he would clean the gas by straining it through cheese cloth. Since we had planned to play golf, I teed up at the fourth hole, pleased at my composure on my first plane ride. That was a delusion. I fanned five times as I tried to drive the ball off the tee. Ted came back with a gallon of gas that he had strained through cheese cloth and poured it in the Jenny.

The two of us climbed in the open cockpit again, and the Jenny moved off slowly down the fairway. I was sure we were about to crash into the trees and telephone poles of Lincoln Highway. Ted yelled,

"Hang on!" Then he must have yanked something. Whatever he did caused the Jenny to pop up fifty feet like a champagne cork to clear the trees. Jenny's engine was still sputtering. Ted tried to restore it to health with steep vertical dives. I kept from falling out of the plane by clutching my seat. Ted yelled that we would have to come down. We descended fast and landed helter-skelter in a cow pasture. Ted climbed on top of the engine and blew into the carburetor.

Just as I, bedazed, was about to crawl out of the cockpit, Ted held up a finger and said, "The wind is right. I think I can try a take-off." The wind lifted Jenny in a fifty-yard take-off. We made it safely to the airport in New Brunswick where we left the plane for repairs. I said good-bye to Jenny gratefully.

Because of that scary ride in the Jenny in 1927, I could not bring myself to fly again for thirty-eight years.

All the Princeton students and townspeople got an extraordinary charge out of the Lindbergh solo flight across the Atlantic. Everybody read all the newspaper stories about his preparations for the flight, how he planned to guide it to the tip of Ireland and on, we hoped, to Le Bourget Field in Paris. We visualized his lonely hours over that vast ocean. It all seemed an incredibly courageous thing to do. It was an immense relief to Princeton when word came that he had arrived at Le Bourget safely on May 20, 1927. Nobody objected when it was reported that *The New York Times* paid him $250,000 for his exclusive account of his flight. The people of St. Louis gave him $50,000 for bringing fame to their city. Princeton students built a huge bonfire in his honor, even bigger than the bonfires built for beating Yale in football.

The students had hardly got over the excitement of Lindbergh's flight when an event happened that they found almost as thrilling. That was a movie at the Garden Theater—Greta Garbo and John Gilbert in a movie called *Flesh and the Devil*. I cannot explain the stunning effect on us of Greta Garbo's beauty. She was just *different* from the Hollywood stars like Pola Negri and Eleanor Boarden. The Garbo film was based on a Russian novel about a soldier (John Gilbert) who sought Greta Garbo's affection. We never saw anything that moved us as much as Greta Garbo's classic profile as she sat blowing smoke into John Gilbert's eager face. I still regard Greta Garbo, who died in 1990, as the most beautiful woman I ever have seen.

I don't know if all this excitement had anything to do with the below-passing marks that I was getting in college algebra. I wrote Uncle Hal in Bridgeport that I was about to flunk out of college. Could he send me $90 to pay the algebra tutor? In his letter with the $90, Uncle Hal wrote, "I never did understand algebra when I was at Yale in 1881." With the help of the Hun School tutor, I passed the algebra exam and thus became a Princeton sophomore.

Chapter Seven

THE FIRST TIME I SAW PARIS

YOU CAN be sure that Jack Howe's six "Tiger Cubs" did arrive on June 16, 1927, at the Cunard dock on 14th Street in New York for the noon sailing of the *S.S. Tuscania*. The dock vibrated with the air of festival that marked the many summer sailings to Europe in the 1920s. The first and second class passengers of the *Tuscania* climbed up the gang plank to the deck followed by a swarm of friends loaded with farewell bottles of champagne and bouquets of flowers to put in their cabins. Their steamer trunks had preceded them.

The Tiger Cubs with their instruments and suitcases climbed with some five hundred Tourist Third students to their quarters in the stern of the *Tuscania*. The band found their double-bunks on F-deck near the salt water shower bath. The bunks were so low down that port holes had to be kept closed to keep the sea water from pouring in on us.

Jack set the band up on a raised hatch of the Tourist Third promenade deck. I checked the little deck piano which had a folding keyboard. The piano was out of tune, but not so badly as some we had which were a whole tone down. That is to say if we were supposed to play in the key of B flat, we would have to play in the key of A. Fortunately we had reached such a level of professionalism that the band could play even in a key we detested, like A.

When the Tuscania's fog horn blew its departure warning, the crowd of visitors disembarked and tugs eased the ship into the Hudson River and headed it south. As the students gathered around the band we greeted the noble Statue of Liberty with up-tempo "Tiger Rag."

Passing Staten Island, we swung into the tune "Collegiate," a Fred Waring tune that I never liked because the lyrics clumsily rhymed "collegiate" with "intermediate." At Coney Island in the Lower Bay of the Hudson, the ship paused at Ambrose Light. The passengers cheered when the river pilot boarded his motor boat to return to New York. He signaled the *Tuscania's* captain his permission to proceed into the Atlantic Ocean on its three thousand-mile ten-day voyage to Europe.

These memories of that sunny day with Ambrose Light and Sanly Hook fading in the sunset lead me to consider how modern technology has robbed all of us today of the delight I experienced in 1927. I am reminded that few people these days cross the Atlantic by ship. Most of the transatlantic ships were sunk by German U-boats during World War II. Travelers to Europe today cross without ever seeing the Atlantic, the most beautiful, dramatic and interesting of all our oceans. They fly across in jumbo jet planes enduring excruciating hours of boredom with nothing to do or see except to crawl past snoring passengers to the restroom only to find it "Occupied."

In contrast travel across the Atlantic by steamship is a joy, a rare experience. That is so even in rough weather, even for people who have a day or two of seasickness. On the ocean crossing one is completely divorced from the problems known on shore; there is freedom from all bothersome things—telephones, people calling about nothing, mail, bills coming in. There is absolutely nothing to do but to enjoy one's serenity.

The 16,000-ton *Tuscania* moved toward Europe at a leisurely pace of ten knots an hour. During our first week at sea, we had perfect weather. The Tiger Cubs played for the students at tea time and again in the evening from about eight to ten.

Each day the Atlantic brought us something exciting—a spouting whale or some playful dolphins swimming alongside the ship, or a flock of gulls followed in the wake of our stern. One day we saw a small iceberg that had floated down from Greenland.

The Tourist Third students seemed to like our music. We played all the tunes of the day such as "Hallelujah," "I Know That You Know," and "The Best Things in Life are Free." The whole band sang tunelessly "Charlie, My Boy" using the song's title for words all the way through. Then Jack would announce solemnly with a roll of the drums,

"Ladies and gentlemen, the name of that song was 'Charlie, My Boy'."
We even played a song I wrote trying to emulate Lawrence Hart's
penchant for rhyming long words.

> I cannot offer an apology
> Because I'm no student of
> psychology
> But I have a notion
> That some revolting potion
> Has altered your devotion
> And caused this strange commotion.
> I may seem harmless
> But that's just a sham;
> I'm really audacious, pugnacious,
> rapacious.
> I can't stand this protraction;
> I love you to distraction,
> But, what's your big attraction
> That's what I'd like to know.

The students did quite a variety of dancing, some of them still dancing the Charleston and others having a stab at the Black Bottom or Big
Apple. Since there was no privacy on the Promenade deck, some tried
to find it by sneaking behind the lifeboats, which was forbidden. There
were no guard rails on that side. The captain was afraid that in a
moment of animal passion, they might fall off the boat into the ocean.

The captain of the *Tuscania* and his English crew liked the students
and spoiled them with special privileges. The captain showed us the
engine room and gave us full run of the ship including the first-class
bar. Jack Howe and I sometimes climbed thirty or forty feet up the
mast to the crow's nest to help the lookout spot oncoming ships. After
our evening dance, some couples found their way to the kitchen where
the chef made roast beef sandwiches and English muffins for them.

As often happens on the temperamental Atlantic Ocean, the ship ran
into a severe storm with high winds. Some of the winds tilted the *Tuscania* at a 35-degree angle, smashing dishes and furniture as they slid
from one side to the other with each roll. The captain steered the ship
southward to miss the force of the storm. As a result we were a day

late approaching France and came into the harbor at Le Havre after dark when customs was closed. Nobody was allowed off the ship until the next morning.

I had my first view of France from the prow of the *Tuscania* before we tied up at the dock. I could see the dancing lights from the cafes along the waterfront. As I looked at it, I felt that peculiar entrancement that many people feel just looking at any part of France. Perhaps that is because people think of its unique quality as one of the world's great centers of art, music, literature, fashion and even scientific achievements. Perhaps the excitement I felt was heightened by my childhood memories of listening to my Aunt Mary's vivid description of Paris during her several visits in the late 1890s and early 1900s.

I had been looking forward to a date I had made for my last night on the boat with an Irish girl from Schenectady. But the girl broke that date at the last minute. She said she wanted to spend that night with a Princeton senior. While I was fretting about that, I noticed that one of our English waiters was climbing down one of the double cables that tied the *Tuscania* to the dock for the night. I followed him creeping down the cable to the dock. The two of us walked on the empty dock a few hundred yards to the line of cafes along the waterfront. The English boy and I went into the cafe and were served beers by a very pretty little French girl. After the beers, the English boy took the girl's hand and the two went upstairs without a word. After fifteen minutes they returned and the girl brought me another beer while rearranging her hair and her dress a bit. Around midnight the English waiter said we should be getting back to the ship. As we walked back he told me what had happened to him when he took the girl upstairs. I was delighted by his story. I had never seen such a thing happen in any saloon in Trenton or New York. So this was France, unreconstructed, as my French teacher at Princeton told me. What a wonderful country, I thought!

The next day we left the ship and rode the boat train from Le Havre through the beautiful French countryside with its vegetable gardens to the Gare St. Lazare where Mother met me. She was staying at the Hotel Chatham. She told me how much she enjoyed writing her fashion reports for *Women's Wear Daily* in New York. I took a night off to visit Harry's New York Bar that I had been told about, the address of which was, people said, "Sank Roo Don't Know" (Cinque Rue Daunou).

Harry's Bar was near the Chatham where I found an old Chicago stride piano player, Glover Compton, entertaining the customers with a song he had written "I Found Romance on the Ile de France." Some nights later I went to Montmartre to Zelli's, a New York style night-club, where I had a glimpse of Buster Keaton hiding in a corner like a frightened mouse. While there, Joe Zelli announced, "One of our customers from Cincinnati has asked us to let her sing to you. Her name is Libby Holman." Libby was a very voluptuous girl. She sang in a loud sultry voice "St. Louis Blues." Two or three years later I went to "The First Little Show" in New York and there was Libby Holman, a famous torch singer singing "Moanin' Low," and "Can't We Be Friends" with Clifton Webb as her boyfriend.

————

I still had some weeks before the *Tuscania* took Jack and the "Tiger Cubs" back to New York in August. Mother took me on a tour of the fashionable resorts that she covered for *Woman's Wear*. I knew it was typical of my mother that the hotel managers like Hans Badrut at St. Moritz gave her free meals and board, in return for the publicity she gave them in *Women's Wear Daily*. Mother and I went to Vichy first. It had a small dance band. I admired the pianist's playing and asked him to give me a lesson to see if he could improve my fingering. I paid him 100 francs for a lesson. In the course of the brief lesson—maybe thirty minutes—he asked me to show him how to play stride piano. Then I spent two hours showing him that—for free.

From Vichy we went on to Biaritz and Baden-Baden in Germany and finally to the famous Palace Hotel in St. Moritz. In the elevator at the Palace, the door opened and a smallish, neat, white-haired man stepped in. I knew he was Fritz Kreisler. I told him that I had heard him in concert way back when my mother took me to concerts in Car-negie Hall. Fritz Kreisler smiled as I spoke. As he left the elevator, he shook my hand. I never forgot that moment. To this day, I often look at my hand and tell myself, "That hand shook the hand of one of the great musicians of the world."

I went by train from St. Moritz to Paris. I stopped at La Boetie Hotel. I was about broke and had to take a cheap room in the attic. I was moping around my room feeling lonely when I heard somebody in the room below. It sounded like someone taking a shower. A voice rang out "March, march, marching for Lawrence wearing the big red L." I didn't feel lonely any more. I found in later years I could find someone from Lawrenceville almost anywhere in the world.

Back in Le Havre I found the band and Jack Howe for the return trip which was nice but uneventful. Jack told me that the purser had told him that he had liked our band on the eastern trip. Would our band play on the *Berengeria*, the flagship of the Cunard line, almost the biggest boat on the Atlantic run, next summer? We were pleased about that. We would return on the Cunard *Cameronia* from Perth, Scotland, and to get us to Perth the Cunard line would pay our passage on the Edinburgh Express, that ran in eight hours nonstop from London to Edinburgh.

Chapter Eight

Princeton Bicker Week

I WAS GLAD to get back from Newark to 66 Nassau to start my sophomore year at Princeton. The Shenks had arrived from their home in Erie, Pennsylvania. We were glad that our freshman year was behind us. We knew we had a busy year ahead of us. The Shenk twins were strong swimmers and would be working as members of the varsity swimming team. I was involved with the activities of the Triangle Club.

To become a member of the Princeton Triangle Club was equivalent in prestige to playing on the football team. The Club was founded in 1891 with Booth Tarkington as one of its founders. In 1893, Booth Tarkington wrote the musical "Julius Caesar." The Club became immensely popular. It spent its Christmas holidays staging its musical show in major cities. The book, music and staging were produced entirely by undergraduates.

Members of the Princeton Triangle Club had an important effect on the Broadway theater and on movies during the 1920s and 1930s. W.H. Smith wrote the successful musical "Drake's Drum." Two of his songs were natural hits—"All the Ships that Pass in the Night" and "Pirate Gold."

Herb Sanford wrote in 1927 the Triangle Club music and the book for *On the Road to Samarkand.* Sanford went on to become a sort of Boswell for modern jazz. He wrote a biography of the Dorsey brothers.

E.H. Herbison wrote the book and some of the music for "Napoleon Passes." The part of Czarina of Russia was played by Phillips

Holmes, who was acclaimed to have been the most beautiful "girl" in Triangle history. In 1931 Holmes went to Hollywood to star in the movie "An American Tragedy." "Napoleon Passes" was written by George Bradshaw, who wrote the dialogue for many Hollywood movies.

Jimmy Stewart, a member of the Triangle Club in 1932 went to Hollywood to star in a hundred exceedingly successful movies. Josh Logan co-authored the Triangle musical "Zuider Zee" in 1931. Later he directed "Mister Roberts," "South Pacific," "Annie Get Your Gun" and "Fannie." He directed several films including "Bus Stop."

Music from the Triangle shows became nationally known, such as the tune "All Ships That Pass in the Night" by W.H. Smith for the 1934 production of "Drake's Drum." In 1935 Brooks Bowman wrote the song "East of the Sun" for "Stags at Bay." This song became a world standard that you can hear today in Tokyo, Australia, Egypt and Paris. Its author Bowman was killed in an auto accident in 1938.

I always envied Jack Howe's musical ability and wished that I was more than a plunkety-plunk piano player. I was pleased when I was asked to supply the piano rhythm for the rehearsals of the twenty-man "Girl" chorus for "Napoleon Passes." The Triangle Club hired Gus Shy, the star comedian of the longrunning musical "Good News" to train the chorus line of "Napoleon Passes." Gus was a joy to work with and he seemed to like my playing. One day, however, he objected to the rhythm of one of the "Napoleon Passes" songs and asked me to give it more of an up tempo. I played "Varsity" Drag from "Good News" and changed the melody into one of my own using the Varsity Drag chord structure. Later the Triangle Club music director picked up my melody and made me a member of the Club with a credit in the program of "Napoleon Passes."

I enjoyed my work for Gus Shy as he trained the chorus line for "Napoleon Passes." I marveled at his good cheer and stamina, working from three to four or five o'clock in the afternoon, then hurrying to New York to appear in the matinee of "Good News." The show went through the Christmas holidays.

When the Shenks returned we had another nerve-racking distraction, Bicker Week, when the sophomores were invited by the three-man Bicker committee of each of Princeton's seventeen eating clubs, all on Prospect Street, to join this or that club. Joining one of the eating clubs would allow us to take our meals on the sacred precincts of Prospect Street. Members of the clubs were selected by a three-member Bicker committee of each club who picked the people they deemed suitable for their club, a most undemocratic process, I always thought. I remember having read that Woodrow Wilson was President of Princeton in 1902 when Princeton abolished national fraternities and that he tried hard to provide a single club called the Quadrangle to which all students were eligible to belong. The trustees and the faculty objected to that democratic solution. They felt they had a right to be exclusive and to form clubs to which they would invite people they liked and from which they could keep out people they didn't like. The result of their efforts was Bicker Week, and that was the busy prospect we had in September 1927.

Meanwhile as the middle of February approached in 1928, Chick and Al and I went into the Bicker Week problem. The Shenks and I took the matter of Bicker Week seriously as did most undergraduates. We realized the importance of being invited into a respectable eating club. The eating clubs were independent of the university. The title of the property of each club was controlled by a board of governors composed of much older Princeton alumni. The university imposed no rules whatever. The members could drink whatever they like and behave any way they liked. They were not governed in any way even during house parties.

We knew very little about the seventeen eating clubs on Prospect Street. I don't remember ever having been in one. What we sophomores knew was mostly gossip and hearsay. We did know that the top club was the oldest club, Ivy Club, founded in 1879. It was our idea, probably most inaccurate, that the fathers of members of Ivy Club were all aristocratic Philadelphians who were descendants of William Penn, the founder of Pennsylvania. Also we understood that the members of Ivy Club held their liquor about as well as Ernest Hemingway. We thought that was a great achievement.

The next oldest club was Cottage Club founded in 1887. It seemed to us that being a member of the Triangle Club chorus paved your way to become a member of Cottage Club. Then, we believed that the third top club was Tiger Inn which was founded in 1892 and usually took most of the athletes, men who had won their varsity letters on the football team, the crew and the like. Another very respectable club was Cap and Gown started in 1894. We believed that members of Cap and Gown had the highest standards of morality of all of us and that they were what we called Princeton's "Christers," which was mean of us, I thought.

After the four, the other seventeen clubs were variously rated. We understood that the wildest house parties in the spring with the best bands were given by Cannon Club and Elm Club. For some reason or other the Shenks and I liked Tower Club, I don't remember why. During our Bicker Week, when the three-man committee came calling, a very formal affairs, we dressed up in jackets and ties and listened anxiously for the sound of their steps coming up the steps to our rooms at 66 Nassau. There they spent a few minutes of looking us over, carrying on a stilted conversation about nothing at all. We thought we had made a fine impression with the Bicker committee from Tower Club. Finally the great day of getting bids arrived in mid-February and we received no bids to become members of Tower Club. We did get bids from Elm and Campus. We were mad as the dickens. So on the day when the sophomores went down Prospect Street to the various clubs to accept the invitations, the Shenks and I walked angrily past Tower Club which had turned us down. As we walked down the street we picked up seventeen friends of ours who had also not been accepted by the Club they preferred. We had a little conference in front of Cap and Gown.

Among us was one of our best friends, Gibby Kane. We wanted Jack Howe but he had accepted the bid of the top-ranked Tiger Inn because he was on the varsity crew as coxswain, as I have explained, because of his rhythmic sense. Next to Cap and Gown was Cloister Inn, a very nice looking Club with a dining room that overlooked a nice sunken garden on the other side. So one of us said, "Let's all go in en masse and offer all seventeen of us." That's what we did. The Bicker committee was there. They hadn't had a very good response to their invitations. They were delighted at our appearance, fearing that they would not have enough members to keep the Club going. They took all seventeen of us sophomores in immediately and that's how we became members of Cloister Inn. The following year the seventeen of us took complete control of the Club with Chick Shenk elected president. We elected Gibby Kane as the Club's manager which gave him free meals for handling the employment of the cook, waiters and housekeeper.

In May, the Shenks and I attended Cloister Inn's spring house party. Each of the seventeen Prospect Street clubs gave these weekend bashes annually. They created a frenzy that was even worse than the proms had been at Lawrenceville. Each club hired small dance bands of free-lance musicians from New York. Jack Howe and I heard all of them to get ideas for our forthcoming job in June on the *S.S. Berengeria*. Members of all the clubs could visit any club to listen to its band. This created a swirl of arm-in-arm party-goers walking on Prospect Street— the girls in evening dress and the men in tuxedos or top hats and tails.

I remember the various bands that year—Key and Seal Club had hired Paul Tremaine's "Lonely Acres" band from the Chinese-American restaurant on Broadway. At Campus Club was Louis Armstrong, down from Fletcher Henderson's Roseland. Armstrong was already being billed as "the world's greatest trumpet player." Canon Club and Cloister Club shared Red Nichols with the legendary Miff Mole on trombone, Arthur Shutt on piano, and the guitarist Eddie Lang. Colonial Club had Ben Bernie's twenty-foot-long xylophone. Colonial had invited Bix Beiderbecke and Frankie Trumbauer but they were busy that week making Victor records for Paul Whiteman.

After the Shenks and I had recovered from house parties, we had to move (including the battered upright piano) out of 66 Nassau Street to rooms the University had assigned to us on campus at 104 Blair Hall. The three small rooms had a tiny fireplace. A friend of the Shenks, Arthur Mizener, lived in the entry next to us. We were in awe of Art who got A-plus grades in his courses and read incomprehensible novels like James Branch Cabell's *Jurgen*.

Blair Hall had an enormous gothic tower like a fortress. I liked to walk through it imagining I was Launcelot about to confer with King Arthur on a battle plan. Our rooms were a mile walk from my meals at Cloister, but it was a beautiful walk under the elms of McCosh Walk to Washington Road and Prospect Street.

I managed to pass my sophomore exams and became a junior. Jack Howe and our Tiger Cub band arrived to board the *S.S. Berengeria* for a second stint of playing our way to France in June of 1928.

Chapter Nine

Trailing Julius Caesar

THERE WE were again, the five Tiger Cubs, in June of 1928, on the Cunard dock in New York ready to climb aboard the *S.S. Berengaria* to play for the Tourist Third students crossing from New York to France. The five of us were really frightened by the immense size of the *Berengaria* which was three times the size of *Tuscania* we had played on the year before. The *Berengaria* was longer than a football field and just about as wide. It seemed likely to crush the huge crowd waiting on the dock for the noon sailing. There were four thousand passengers, the purser told us, and fifteen hundred Tourist Third students plus a mob of visitors waiting to say goodbye when the ship departed for France. The *Berengaria* purser told us that the ship was fully booked for the trip. He added, "Don't you believe that all these people were there because of their yearning to visit the cultural sights of France and England!" In recent months all of the Atlantic steamers had noted big business because Americans had become so disillusioned with Prohibition that they flocked to the foreign ships where they could get a decent drink. There was no Prohibition on the *Berengaria* even in New York as long as the drinks were served on the ship.

Before we left I had looked up the history of the *Berengaria* in the Princeton Firestone library. It had been built as the *Imperator* in 1912 by Kaiser Wilhelm II who intended it to challenge the biggest English boats like the *Mauretania* and its launching had been a national holiday with all the government officials and royalty aboard wearing their spiked helmets. Already the Kaiser was planning to expand his military strength which, of course, led eventually to World War I. After World War I the *Imperator* was given to England in the reparations settlement of the Versailles Treaty. At that same time the big German ship *Leviathan* was given to the United States as part of their reparations. The English took the *Imperator* and spent a great deal of money converting it for its English passenger trade removing all the German signs including the *zigarren* label on its ashtrays and making a huge ballroom out of one of the dining rooms. It had been a four-stacker, but the English removed the aft stack to increase its speed to about twenty-four knots an hour. It was converted to oil. The English changed its name from the *Imperator* to the *Berengaria* in honor of Queen Berengaria who was the wife of Richard the Lion-Hearted, the great English ruler of about 1100. Berengaria was the daughter of the king of Navarro which was in northern Spain and a little bit in France. Richard the Lion-Hearted died young, but his queen spent very little time in England. She retired for most of her later years in La Mans, France, not far from Cherbourg, where the *Berengaria* was scheduled to land in France.

We got on the ship. We played on a raised hatch as we had on the *Tuscania*. We played many of the same tunes of the day, "I'll Get By," "I Can't Give You Anything But Love," and a tune copied from one of the records Rudy Vallee had made when he was a sophomore at Yale, "You'll Do It Someday, So Why Not Now." I don't mean to complain about the *Berengaria* but it really was not as much fun as the *Tuscania*, partly because it was a six-day boat. That wasn't enough time for the students to get acquainted. Then the crew didn't have the time to spoil us as they had on the *Tuscania*. We didn't go down to the kitchen for roast beef sandwiches and muffins the way we had. Jack Howe and I never dreamed of climbing the crow's nest which rose into the stratosphere. It was fun playing for a larger audience, though. The first-class passengers had a way of coming in to hear our music and to dance. The captain didn't give us the run of the ship; we weren't allowed to go out of our Tourist Third quarters in the bow of the boat. The whales and dolphins kept out of our way. We didn't see any other Atlantic steamers passing by. They gave us a wide berth so we wouldn't run into them.

At Cherbourg we got on the train to Paris. I enjoyed the rail trip from Cherbourg to the Gare St. Lazare in Paris and noticed all the apple trees on the way through Normandy. The waiter in the dining car told us that the big product there was a brandy called Calvados. I tasted it and asked him what it was. He told me it was a French version of applejack, but believe me, it tasted a lot different from the applejack that had about killed us during Prohibition at Princeton.

We got to Paris. For some days the five of us had discussed not staying in Paris for the couple of months before we were due to go to Edinburgh and catch the *Cameronia* in Perth, Scotland. We wanted to see something of France. We decided to get some bicycles. We discussed the plan at Harry's New York Bar. Harry's bar was the only place to get milk you dared to drink. Frenchmen preferred to drink *vin ordinaire* instead of milk or water, both of which required boiling to be safe. A couple of years earlier Harry had found a milkman who could deliver milk tested for purity. Harry McElhone was a genial Scotsman who had been a bartender at Ciro's restaurant in London and had opened his bar in Paris in 1923 after checking the look of a few bars in New York on Third Avenue. He made the decor of his bar exactly like one he examined in New York, so when homesick Americans came to Paris they would feel at home. The result was an immensely popular place for Americans right from the start. It was in the center of Paris near the Rue de la Paix where all the fancy jewelry was sold, and not far from the entrance to the Ritz Hotel and Hotel Chatham where Mother usually stayed. We told Harry about our idea of bicycling around France. He rented some bicycles for us.

I had a yen to see southern France because I had read in Caesar's *Commentaries* about how Caesar had conquered Gaul in 52 B.C. We went to the Gare de Lyon, got tickets for a train going south. I was stammering trying to remember enough French that Mr. Wilder had taught me at Lawrenceville to explain where we wanted to go. Like many French ticket takers, he was irritated by us and had that pained expression that Frenchmen always have on their faces whenever an American tries to talk high school French. While we were talking, an English-speaking bystander came up and said he had noticed our bikes. He asked what we were doing. I explained our idea. He said, "That's a fine idea. I'll tell you what you guys do. I know just the trip for you. Go down south to Avignon which was where the popes had their palaces, then to Carcassonne, one of the first places Caesar had gone to. From there, ride across beautiful level country (the weather will be just right for you) and visit the other towns Caesar had set up after his conquest of southern France near the Mediterranean. When you are in Avignon you will see the famous bridge built by the popes. Another interesting historical site in Avignon is the red light district which, I've been told, was started to serve the soldiers in the French Army. The architecture, the line of cribs of red brick, was done by one of the pope's architects." We were grateful for our friend's advice. We did go by train to Avignon on the Rhone. We found a hotel for fifty cents each per night. After supper someone showed us how to get to the famous antique red light district. Sure enough, outside where the red bricks of the cribs were, was a large red light to make sure you knew what the place was. The five of us walked through. It was quite depressing. The girls were all shouting at us. They sounded like they were in their teens and didn't have enough to eat. We hurried and were glad to leave the line of cribs, seventy or eighty yards long. We went back to our hotel and to bed planning to go to Carcassonne the next morning.

By five o'clock we found out why that hotel was so cheap. The bed bugs had just about eaten us up. We were all awake, so we got up, went to the railroad station, got third class tickets on a train to Carcassonne. Our car was full of white leghorn chickens that were being sent to Bordeaux beyond Carcassonne. We had a nice ride to Carcassonne and spent a couple of days in that ancient town, one of the first towns walled for protection from attack by the Visigoths and the Saracens that Julius Caesar cleaned out of the region. It was a wonderful place to imagine Caesar with his horses and soldiers around 52 B.C. beginning his career taking over all of Europe for Rome.

After we left Carcassone we took a beautiful road across southern France. We found we could do about one hundred kilometers a day or about sixty miles on our bikes without too much trouble. The first town was Narbonne about five miles from the Mediterranean which we could see from the road. There were vineyards along the way. On one of the hotter days our drummer had a fainting spell. That worried us greatly. We got him under a tree, threw water on him and revived him. After an hour or so he seemed to recover so we went on to the university town of Montpelier. It reminded me of Princeton with the row of faculty homes. I noticed later that Montpelier, Vermont, was named after that town in France.

There is an airy gentle quality about southern France that makes you feel lucky to be alive. Two gendarmes arrested us for not having licenses for bicycles. They were good-natured and enjoyed letting us take pictures of them seeming to beat us with their batons.

We didn't have time to find out what we were looking at. But we were impressed by the antiquity, the varieties of rulers represented: Caesar, of course, minor counts, small kingdoms, even the wife of the count of Burgundy who had a town named Beatrice to herself.

Finally we came to the most incredible treasure of them all, the old town of Nimes, not a large place, about thirty thousand people. It had an amazing assortment of every kind of antiquities, all of which had survived battles with the Visigoths, Saracens, Crusaders, Catholics, Napoleon, the Romans, the Germans, the Protestants and various kingdoms and counts. I will not pretend I knew the complicated history then, but I read about it many years later. As we rode through that history on our trip it was more than we could grasp.

Nimes is a tremendous walled city with a huge amphitheater, built by the Romans, which seats twenty thousand people, and was used by gladiator spectacles and chariot races and bullfights. While we were there, they had a bullfight. They did not kill the bull as in Spain. I was glad the French didn't permit the bull to be killed. I kept thinking how glad I was that Grandmother Osburn wasn't there as she loved her cows so and wouldn't have dreamed of having them hurt in any way.

We planned to go from there down a long hill to Marseilles heading for the Riviera along the Corniche. We went slowly, got picked up by some American tourists and given a sumptuous feast in view of the Mediterranean. They treated us royally with dinner, lots of champagne and talk. We continued through Nice and on to Monte Carlo, a gem of a city, incredibly beautiful and manicured. Every flower looked as if it had been planted that day.

So getting a little tired of our bike riding, we took the train from Monaco to Milan and then got on one of those tiny Swiss electric trains which carried us northward into the beautiful Alps of Switzerland starting with Lugano, then moving on to that picturesque little town Vevey and then Lausanne and continued on. This whole trip only took a day. We didn't see much except the scenery from the train. We went on and the train continued to Karlsruhe, a fairly large industrial city on the Rhine River. We took our bikes off and began riding down the

Rhine. Such a beautiful river, but we were absolutely astonished by the amount of traffic on it as it was the main artery for business and tourism in Germany all the way from the English Channel. It carried all the traffic of the Netherlands, Belgium and Italy. The river was amazingly full of every kind of craft although it was a fairly large river, as large in places as the Hudson, but, of course, not nearly as long as the Mississippi. It was a beautiful ride down on the east bank where we could see the various castles. We went through the cities of Koblenz, Bonn and Köln (Cologne). I can't remember what we thought about the architecture of the churches. It seems to me that they didn't compare with the graceful quality of the French cathedrals. They had a kind of stolid, almost militant look, like the German people. They gave us the feeling when we talked to them that America was nothing very spectacular because the Germans were so wonderful in every way.

We got to our hotel in Koblenz. The hotel manager asked us to have dinner with him because he wanted to ask about some relatives of his who were running a beer garden in New York on 86th Street and 3rd Avenue. He seemed to be a little bit worried. While we were talking at dinner, he asked rather quietly, as though he didn't want anybody else to hear, if we had ever heard of a book called *Mein Kampf* (*My Struggle*) by a lately rising politician named Adolf Hitler. His book published in 1927 had not been read very much, but when Hitler began to rise politically and promote his book it began to sell like mad. Millions of Germans read it. The German told us in guarded fashion that the book worried him because Hitler said plainly that he intended to ignore all the terms of the 1921 Versailles Treaty at the conclusion of World War I, to rearm Germany and eventually recover all the territories that Germany had lost by the Versailles Treaty. Hitler was getting a great response from the German people and was forming a large body of militant followers called brown shirts, thousands of them all over Germany. Then he asked me what would Americans think about this. Did they know about Hitler? Were they talking about him? Were they worried about him? He said, "Well, I'm worried about him because I just don't know how it will affect the summer business of my hotel. If my English-speaking customers read it and find out his intentions, they may not come and see me in the summer. I certainly need their business."

We kept his remarks in mind as we continued our ride to Cologne. The German people did seem to be rather anxious about something;

we didn't know exactly what it was. We left Jack Howe and the members of the Tiger Cubs who returned their bicycles in Paris and then planned to go to London in time to catch the *Cameronia* from Edinburgh, Scotland, towards the middle of August. That was the time we were to return to New York. In the meantime I took off to Hamburg, Germany, to spend a couple of days with my sister Josie whose husband Howie Taylor, after serving as commercial attache in Stuttgart for the American consulate, had been transferred to Hamburg in the same position. He had been told that in a year or two he might be transferred to a post in China as commercial attache. I had to get moving to join my band in London, so Howie arranged my passage on the Hamburg-America liner *New York* from Breman. After a day I arrived in Southhampton and found Jack Howe and the rest of the band in London at the Hotel St. James near Hyde Park.

They told me that during the few days they were there they had seen a musical comedy with a girl named Gertrude Lawrence starring in it. They remembered that she had starred on Broadway in 1926 in the George Gershwin musical comedy "Okay." She sang a song that Jack Howe thought a lot of. It had never been published. It had been written by Johnny Green, a Harvard man. The song was "Coquette." Gertrude Lawrence would become as popular as Marilyn Miller had been in the years before. They had heard her sing another song that Jack Howe liked. The song "Body and Soul" had not been published, but Jack found out later it also had been written by Johnny Green, Gertrude Lawrence's accompanist. Bert Ambrose, the most popular jazz band in London at the time, was playing it. Jack, with his phenomenal musical memory and his perfect pitch, knew they were playing it in A flat, and he wrote parts for the rest of the band. He even had the correct weird chord changes. That's how it happened that when we got on the *Cameronia* we were able to play "Body and Soul" that wouldn't be heard in America for another year or two. When it was played it became an instant smash hit and is still heard almost as often as Brooks Bowman's "East of the Sun."

The band got our Cunard passages on the nonstop train "The Flying Scot" from London to Edinburgh in good time. We made our way to the harbor at Perth where the *Cameronia* was docked. We boarded the ship and began setting up the band on a raised hatch. (It was about the size of the *Tuscania* and didn't have a very large crowd of Tourist Third on it.) All of a sudden the captain came up and said, "What do you men think you're doing here?" Jack said, "Well, we're the band that the Cunard line signed up to play for Tourist Third on the way back to New York." The captain said, "I never received any such word from the Cunard line. Let me hear you play." We played him "Tiger Rag" with fervor; getting home depended on this. When we finished the Captain grinned and said, "Bravo, lads. That sounds pretty good, but I'd like it better if you played it on bagpipes. We will assign you cabins. We'll take your word for it."

In the middle of August I went home to Newark to tell Dad and Aunt Mary of our adventures on the bicycle trip before getting back to our new rooms at 104 Blair at Princeton for the start of my senior year.

Chapter Ten

IN MAINE WITH WATER LILY

IN SEPTEMBER 1928, I joined the Shenk twins at our new campus digs at 104 Blair Hall to start our junior year.

I don't remember much about that year except that I spent most of the time worrying about everything. I worried that my low C average in my English major might be too low for me to graduate with the class of 1930. I wondered how Dad would feel about scraping up enough money to pay my annual Princeton tuition of $1200 plus the cost of my meals for a year at Cloister Inn only to find that his son had nothing to show for that expense except a liberal education in jazz.

I had resumed plunking out the rhythm for the "girls" chorus of the 1928 Triangle Club musical "Zuider Zee." I enjoyed watching the boys with their hairy legs trying to kick high and in general act as though they were girls. One day DeFord Swan came to a chorus rehearsal. He was a fine jazz piano player and was director of the pit orchestra for "Zuider Zee." I stepped away from the piano to let DeFord play a little. He played a tune that I did not recognize, but I thought it was delightful. It was George Gershwin's "The Man I Love." It would become one of several popular songs with a beauty of melody and lyrics that I would always find delightful, and it would stay with me for life.

Gershwin had written "The Man I Love" in 1924 for the vaudeville team of Adele Astaire and Fred Astaire, her brother, to use in the great musical "Lady Be Good." "The Man I Love" had a marvelous ingenious middle part. It was dropped from that show as being uninteresting. The song was dropped again in 1930 from "Strike Up the Band." So that immortal song was never thought good enough for use in a Broadway show.

Jack Howe and our "Tiger Cubs" dance band received a low blow that fall to worry me when a piano-playing freshman from Puerto Rico stole our monthly job playing for the girls at Miss Fine's school in Princeton. This upstart freshman named Jose Ferrer was given a part in the Triangle musical with another freshman Jimmy Stewart. Both went on to become stars. Ferrer won acclaim on the stage by playing the wily Iago for Paul Robeson's "Othello."

A minor worry after Christmas occurred when Jack Howe's "Tiger Cubs" were hired to play for a debutante ball in the glamorous St. Regis Roof. We played that job all right expecting to be paid $40 per man which was the highest price any of us had ever been paid for playing. The trouble was that we never got that money because the man who sold the tickets to the debutantes took off with all the money and went to Montreal and was never seen again.

During that winter I worried because I seemed to be losing weight. I had gone down to about 128 pounds. Also I was having periods of fatigue, and I found it tiring to walk the mile from 104 Blair to Prospect Street for meals.

In March of 1929 Jack Howe told me that he had a full-time summer job for the "Tiger Cubs" playing for a resort in Wisconsin. I told Jack that I didn't think I had better go with him. I didn't feel up to it, so Jack got another piano player for the summer. But I wondered what I would do with myself.

One day in April one of the alumni residents, Bob Denniston, stopped in for lunch at Cloister Inn. After lunch I had gone to our piano upstairs in the club. Bob Denniston came and sat down near the piano. I began playing one of the tunes I had written which the Triangle Club had turned down. I sang it softly. The words went something like this:

> Sing a song of summer
> sunny skies above,
> There is nothing dumber
> if you're not in love.
> Let's be sentimental,
> let's stop being frank,

let's keep our illusions
just like money in the bank.
Ganders love their geeses
and I love you to pieces.
Sing a song of summertime.

When I stopped playing Bob Denniston got up from his chair and come over to the piano. He said, "As I listened to you playing, I had a great idea. What would you think about coming to a boy's camp in Maine in June as the camp's entertainment director. You would handle the nightly singing around the campfire and maybe help us put on a little show for the people living in the camp's neighborhood." I said, "Well, Bob, that sounds like great to me. I have always heard a lot about the delights of Maine and always wanted to see it. Maybe after a summer there, I would gain weight and prepare myself for my senior year at Princeton." So it was decided that I would take the job.

I went to Grand Central Station in June where I found Bob Denniston and fifteen or twenty boys, most of them from Scarborough School in Westchester County, New York. The boys were ages eight to sixteen or seventeen. Three of them were members of one family named Ailes in Scarborough. They were there with their beautiful white-haired mother Mrs. Sallie Ailes. Steve Ailes, the oldest, was about seventeen. Trouble Ailes was fifteen. His name was John, but he had been nicknamed by the Ailes cook who always said of him that whenever he came into the kitchen, "Here comes Trouble." Geno Ailes was about twelve. The Ailes' daughter, Annie, would come with us, too, to stay with Mrs. Sue Snyder. Her husband, Roy Snyder, had started the camp with Bob on Nicatous Lake in Main, having bought an old hunting resort there. The boys and I got into the Nicatous Pullman car on the Boston and Maine Railroad. We went to Bangor, Maine. From there a bus took us some thirty miles along the Penobscot River to a little mill town called Passadumkeag. All of those little Maine towns were named for Algonquin Indians who settled the area long before the French and the English arrived in the 1600s. From Passadumkeag we rode about thirty miles on a horrendously rough plank road into the forest to stop on the shore of one of the loveliest bodies of water I have ever seen. Nicatous Lake was about eleven miles long and a mile wide with several log cabins around one end and a larger house where the meals were served.

I can think of no time in my life that I enjoyed more than those two months on that delightful lake. It was just pure joy. We had a little dock we called the toothbrush dock where we washed after breakfast. It was on a little stream where we did our swimming and racing.

We had two wonderful Maine guides to teach us how to behave ourselves in Maine. If there are people in the world more fun to be with than Maine guides, I have never met them anywhere. They loved their lives, simple as their lives are. They had no interest in the kind of success most people wear themselves out trying to attain. During those weeks at the camp my health improved tremendously, and my outlook, too.

In the middle of August I put together a little show if you could call it that. It was supposed to be based on Maine's Algonquin history. I cast Steve Ailes as the big Indian Chief Iron Stomach who created tense drama by pressing his licentious attentions on an innocent little Indian girl named Water Lily. To save Water Lily from Iron Stomach's evil designs, I directed Water Lily, played by Trouble Ailes, to keep a distance from him. One stage direction read "Enter the Cringing Waterlily." For the rest of his career as a distinguished lawyer and newspaper editor, some of Trouble Ailes's friends called him "The Cringing Water Lily." Steve Ailes, even when he became President Lyndon Johnson's Secretary of the Army, was known behind his back at the Pentagon as Iron Stomach. My dramatic play was well received by residents of the Nicatous area.

The three Ailes boys had been telling me all summer that they had a sister named Edna Jane, or, as they called her, EJ, who would be a junior at Vassar. They seemed to think she was an attractive girl, but mostly they bragged about her ability at football and baseball. All the brothers were dying for me to meet her and find out what I thought of this remarkable person. They said she was coming up with their mother to take them home when camp ended in August.

So it happened that I was curious about this girl named Edna Jane or EJ. Sure enough she came with her mother in a new 1930 La Salle. My first reaction was rather negative, I hate to say. She was wearing high heels, and I was wearing sandals. I said, "O, my God, she is taller than I am." I always hated tall girls because being small myself I didn't want to be manhandled by a woman since I was manhandled enough as it was. EJ otherwise was everything her brothers had said. She was a very trim brown-haired girl. I enjoyed looking at her. She had a profile not quite as classic as Greta Garbo's, but almost so. There was a certain no-nonsense quality that made me feel that I had better not try any monkey business with Edna Jane Ailes, but we got along fine.

I watched her fly-casting a little bit. I was astonished at the marvelous way she could fly-cast with the fly right on the spot where there was a rise immediately without disturbing the trout. She caught a white perch in the very spot where I had tried to catch something for weeks with no luck.

Then I invited her for a canoe ride. We talked a little about Vassar. She wasn't sure she liked it very much. It wasn't long before I asked her to come to my senior prom at Princeton in October. She said she would think about it. I wanted to show her how well Earl Harriman had taught me to paddle. I was paddling away and a little wind came up just enugh so that I couldn't get the canoe turned around into the wind to get back to shore. The wind kept shifting me back again. Finally EJ turned around and said, "Hand me that paddle, please." I gave it to her and in two seconds she had the canoe around, and we were headed smoothly to shore. That didn't please me very much either, but I liked the sound of her voice which was soft and musical. Everything about her was pretty, but I was not ready to admit yet that she was beautiful.

She was telling me about golf, that she had shot an 88. I never shot anywhere near that.

When the camp was over, she and her mother and the boys went away in the La Salle. I went back to New York. Since Mother wasn't back yet from Paris, Sallie Ailes asked me up to Scarborough for the weekend. I went up on the New York Central and found that the whole family had been spending the summer at the Sleepy Hollow Country Club in Scarborough. It was an elegant country club about seven times bigger than the modest Mound Builders Country Club in Newark.

Her father's nickname was "Soldier." EJ told me that he got that nickname because he had enlisted in the Spanish American War. He had gone to Nome, Alaska, as an assayer for New York banks that were buying Nome gold. After that he had met the well-known financier Frank Vanderlip, a millionaire who had a large estate called Beechwood near Scarborough and near the school which Vanderlip had built. Soldier Ailes was sort of a protégé of Vanderlips's, although he later went into a Wall Street brokerage firm.

EJ took me to see the remodeling of their new house, a big beautiful place with a third story with rooms for all the children. It sat on a bluff facing a cove of the Hudson River just above the New York Central commuter station.

I met their cook and the cook's daughter, a household helper, and Harry, Soldier's chauffeur. They also had a year-round gardener taking care of the twenty acres around the house. I was pretty appalled by the elaborate setup. "These people are too much for a boy from Newark, Ohio, whose father earned only $100 a month running the Sprague Grocery Company in Newark," I said to myself.

But I still thought EJ was pretty nice, and I must say she was casual about all the signs of affluence. She was such a gentle girl that I really began to look forward to having her come to my senior prom at Princeton.

Chapter Eleven

GAUDEAMUS

C HICK AND ALLAN SHENK and I were astonished at how quickly the time had passed since we started our junior year, compared to the eternity it seemed to us as freshmen when we faced the years ahead. Seniors at Princeton had certain pleasant perquisites. One of them was that Jack Honore, the college barber, got around to calling seniors by our first names as he doused our heads with his patented hair tonic called Oleaqua.

It was the custom of seniors to gather in the evenings on the steps of Nassau Hall facing the street and singing "Going Back to Nassau Hall" and other old Princeton songs like "Crash Through That Line of Blue." Seniors were allowed to wear beer suits to classes instead of coats and ties. These beer suits were white overall-like canvas affairs. On the back of them each class stenciled a slogan signifying its distinction from all other classes.

Perhaps I should mention here that my class of 1930 may have been more cynical in its outlook than the average class. For one thing we were sick of Prohibition and bootleggers and of big time financiers that were corrupt. Some of the bestselling books of the time were W. E. Woodward's book titled *Bunk* and Oswald Spengler's *The Decline of the West* which gave us the impression that American business was a gigantic shell game with Wall Street brokers manipulating the shells. We were not too surprised, therefore, when the Wall Street Crash of October 1929 occurred. We wondered how the crash would affect us after graduation in getting jobs. Some of our classmates had to leave college because their fathers were not able to pay their tuition. The last straw to our discontent came that fall when Yale clobbered us 18-0 in football. In place of a victory bonfire, we put new stenciled slogans on the back of our beer shirts reading "Bitched All Around." I should have added when I was talking about the things that made us unhappy, that the national hero was John Dillinger, a murderer.

I received several letters from Edna Jane saying that she had decided to come to my senior prom and was worried about whether she had the right clothes and whether I would forget to meet her when she arrived or leave her stranded on the dance floor with no partner.

What made that fall so pleasant was that EJ's mother Sallie invited me to the Ailes' home in Scarborough. I think she thought that I was an abandoned child since Mother was still in Paris working for *Women's Wear Daily*. I remember especially Thanksgiving dinner with the whole Ailes family and EJ's father, Soldier, presiding over the huge turkey in a grand manner sharpening his big knives at the table. I was never sure what Soldier Ailes thought of me, though he was always pleasant. I remember one day outside the house, I climbed a tree and got stuck there and had to call the boys to get me down. Soldier stood under the tree, and I heard him say not quietly, "Does anybody smell skunk around here?" That remark would be repeated thousands of times in years to come.

During that same weekend, Sallie Ailes told me that Soldier was busy with his annual butchering. It seemed that he fattened four or five hogs behind the barn and brought his old friends from Sidney, Ohio, along with several somewhat bewildered Wall Street cronies, to help with the butchering. Sallie laughingly said, "you can take the boy out of the farm. . . ." And so I found that I had lost my feeling about the sophistication of the Ailes. Soldier was a boy from an Ohio farm just as I was a boy from a small Ohio town.

I did meet EJ on time at Princeton Junction. I remember how I admired her graceful walk, not arrogant or belligerent, but confident and smiling, when she stepped off the first car behind the engine and began walking toward me down the long brick platform. I took her to Gibby's car. Students at Princeton were not allowed to have cars, but Gibby Kane could have one because student managers of clubs were allowed to have cars and so were the managers of the football team.

I was afraid that I didn't do very well by EJ at the senior prom in the big gym. I stood in front of the band most of the time as I was fascinated by the music of Roger Wolfe Kahn's large dance band. However, the Shenk twins took good care of Edna Jane, so she was not stranded. Roger Wolfe Kahn was a tiny twenty-one-year-old son of Otto Kahn, the wealthy financier who kept the Metropolitan Opera afloat for years. Roger Wolfe Kahn was a musical prodigy. He could play eighteen jazz instruments including the clarinet which he played very well. He also composed songs, one of them being "Crazy Rhythm" which became a classic. Another tune he wrote was "Following You Around." His band was called the Millionaires Band because every musician had brand new instruments bought by Roger Wolfe Kahn's father. He also had in his band most of the finest jazz musicians of that period including Miff Mole, the star trombone player, and Joe Venutti, the incredible jazz fiddle player, and Eddie Lang, the guitar player whose playing taught the fine guitarists of the 1950s like Johnny Smith and Barney Kettle how to do it.

I was very proud of EJ's appearance at that junior prom. I thought that she was far more attractive than any of the other girls there including the Hollywood movie star Betty Bronson who starred because she believed in fairies in *Peter Pan,* the play by James M. Barrie. I was grateful to Betty Bronson for giving me a solution to my problem of what to write about for my senior English thesis, which I decided might as well be James M. Barrie because I too believed in fairies. So I went ahead that spring and did get my English thesis written just about the time my next door friend Art Mizener was finishing his thesis.

After Christmas for reasons I have never been able to understand, EJ and I began to write to each other much more often, sometimes twice a week. I thought that EJ's letters were extremely well written. She even sent poetry sometimes. We found a mutual interest in novels. Both of us had read the sensation of the day, Thomas Wolfe's *Look Homeward, Angel.* Both of us were overwhelmed with the beauty of Thomas Wolfe's prose and wrote to each other the lines from one of the chapters. "O lost, and by the wind grieved, ghost, come back again." We thought those lines compared favorably with Thomas Gray's classic poem about the churchyard.

As a result of EJ's skill in letter writing, I was encouraged to write better myself to keep up with her. The result of my efforts to write better began to show up in Willard Thorpe's English classes. Dr.

Thorpe began reading some of my short essays to the whole class to show them what could be done with a subject. So you see, writing letters to EJ caused me to forget about jazz and my worries about getting a job, and return to my old dream of being a writer someday.

What scared me a little bit was that our letters began to sound almost like we were falling in love. My suspicions about falling in love were increased when EJ invited me to attend her junior prom at Vassar, and I promised to go. EJ insisted that I drive up thirty miles or so to Poughkeepsie from Scarborough in Soldier's new LaSalle automobile. I drove the LaSalle and that day happened to produce a terrible blizzard. I was scared to death trying to keep the LaSalle on the road. As a result I arrived at Poughkeepsie a nervous wreck. I was bothered all the way there by a feeling I had forgotten something—a tie or something. I survived the nerve-wracking experience of trying to live up to EJ's hopes that her girl friends would admire her prom partner. She seemed to be a bit subdued that evening, gorgeous in a white satin dress with a train that she looped around her with a string on one finger. Then suddenly I remembered what I had forgot. I had forgotten to bring her a corsage—all the other girls had corsages—and EJ had counted on the one I would bring in her choice of her Saks Fifth Avenue silk dress on which the corsage would be the *pièce de résistance.*

My revived interest in writing did not seem to help my low C average in my English major. Meanwhile, in the middle of May Dad wrote me that he and Aunt Mary had decided to come to my graduation in June. I arranged for them to stay in one of the faculty houses and have their meals at Cloister Inn. So it was a tremendous relief to me when the list of the graduating class of 1930 was posted and my name was among them even though I still had a low C average.

A few days after the posting a telegram came from Sallie Ailes saying that she had read in *The New York Times* the list of 1930 Princeton graduates that I had graduated with honors. I just couldn't believe that, but I rushed over to Skirm's Smoke Shop and got a copy of the *Times.* Sure enough, there I was, an honor student, though not high honors, but still an honor student. I couldn't understand how that happened.

To celebrate my good fortune I went to the Kingston Beer Hall near Princeton and was impelled after a few beers to head for Scarborough to tell Edna Jane all about my graduation. I took a taxi and on the way the driver picked up a pedestrian who said his name was James Boyd. I had just been reading in Willard Thorpe's English class Boyd's best seller novel, *Drums,* about North Carolina during the Civil War. I told Boyd about it, and also about my plans to go to see my girl that night whereupon Boyd pulled out his wallet and gave me a twenty-dollar bill to make sure, he said, that I got there safely. "Us Princetonians, you know, have to stick together." Then the two of us burst into a rather raucous version of "Going Back to Nassau Hall."

Between verses Boyd told me he was visiting his best friend on Hodge Road in Princeton, Hugh McNair Kahler who was a well-known short-story writer for *The Saturday Evening Post.* Still singing we pulled into the Kahler driveway, and Mr. Kahler, a tall, slender man, came storming out yelling at us to stop making so much noise. "And who, may I ask, is this drunken bum, this drunken student you are with?" Boyd said, "Well, he's a friend of mine. I just gave him twenty dollars to get to New York with." Kahler said to me, "Now look here, young man, you get that twenty dollars back to me the first thing tomorrow or I'll report your panhandling to Dean Gauss." Of course, that scared me to death, so you can be sure that I mailed him the twenty dollars with a note of thanks. Next day I got a letter from Hugh Kahler reading something like "There's something about the way you phrased that letter that convinced me that you may have natural talent for writing. I intended to see that you become a writer. So, come around, and we'll talk it over. I'll show you how it is done." James Boyd had told me earlier that Hugh Kahler had made him write his novel *Drums* and had been a big help to him in sharing his knowledge of the book publishing business.

So with Dad and Aunt Mary, I attended commencement in front of Nassau Hall under those beautiful trees facing Nassau Street. I listened, trying to keep from falling asleep as President John Greer Hibben droned off the names of all the graduates, the Bachelors of Arts and the Bachelors of Science. I was just about asleep when President Hibben launched into the special honors in architecture, biology, classics and economics and English. Suddenly I woke up as he said, "The Taylor Bond 1859 Honor Prize for English Thesis, Arthur Moore Mizener. Honorable Mention: Marshall Sprague." Well, I just could not believe my ears. I glanced over at Aunt Mary sitting very straight and looking exactly like Queen Mary with a wide smile on her aged face. Dad was smiling, too, as he patted my knee.

With commencement over, I arrived on June 17th at the Cunard Line's 14th Street dock and boarded the *S. S. Lancastria* with Jack Howe's "Tiger Cubs" to play for Tourist Third on a Mediterranean and Norway cruise. The sixty-five-day cruise ended in late August on a Fjord at Narvik above Oslo whence the *Lancastria* returned the band to New York.

Aunt Mary, aged eighty-one, had written a letter to me before we sailed. It read:

Dear Marshall, For our visit at Princeton I want to send thanks to our host for that occasion. I felt I was a girl again, wide as the interval has been between those days and these. The only diploma I ever received was dated 1868. This isn't very clear, but you can guess my meaning. Be a good boy and find a path to happiness when your cruise is over. With love, Mary."

Chapter Twelve

BROTHER, CAN YOU SPARE A DIME

WHEN THE *S. S. Lancastria* returned Jack Howe's "Tiger Cubs" to New York after our two-month jaunt, I decided at once to start looking for a job. I had decided that I had to cease having Dad support me after the expense of five years at Lawrenceville and four years at Princeton.

So I got a cheap room at the Shelton Hotel on Lexington Avenue because I had some money left over from the graduation presents that Uncle Hal and Dad had given me in June. As I walked the pavements of New York in my job quest, I found that September 1930 was the low point of the Great Depression. There simply were no jobs then. That was the worst year of economic crisis in American history. I began pacing the sidewalks of New York, up and down, all the way from 104th Street down to Wall Street. I applied for work at book publishers, banks and advertising agencies.

I had at first tried to stay at 126 West 104th Street while Mother was still working in Paris, but soon found it too depressing at night with the loud arguments of people around who were jobless and frustrated. Sometimes women screamed that they were dying and unable to pay for a doctor. I became terribly depressed those weeks of job hunting by the throngs of panhandlers on the sidewalks and, downtown, people in chairs with little stands of apples and tin cups held out. Further on were the Salvation Army's soup kitchens with long lines of whole families, men, women and children, standing for two or three blocks waiting for a cup of soup to get them through the day.

I did find time in my wanderings to stop in to see Hugh Kahler's literary agent, Carl Brandt, whose office was on the sixth floor of 101 Park Avenue across the street from the Princeton Club of New York. I liked Carl Brandt at first sight. He was about Hugh Kahler's age and much the same in temperament. I saw him very briefly. He talked to me about writing and asked me to send him some short stories which he would submit to his brother Irv Brandt, fiction editor at *The Saturday Evening Post,* who would give him an appraisal of them.

I certainly never expected to emerge after the glory of graduation only to apply myself to finding a job when other people had no use for all the talents I assumed I must have as a graduate. I found the streets as I wandered around the sidewalks cold and disheartening.

In the meantime President Hoover's administration seemed unable to think of anything to do with this crisis except to assure us that everything would return to normal if we were just patient for a while. Nobody dared suggest any kind of public welfare. That would be socialism of the kind advocated by that perennial presidential aspirant Norman Thomas who was head of the Socialist Party and ran for president in 1928 and would probably be running again in 1932.

In September I at last found an offer of a job, not through Princeton which had no employment agency, but from the Yale employment office who said I could have a job selling at Bamberger's Department Store in Newark, New Jersey at $25 a week. I could have that job if I paid the agency $25. I wasted no time getting into my best clothes and riding the Hudson tubes to Newark from Pennsylvania Station and meeting the employment manager at Bamberger's who did hire me to sell drapery goods on the sixth floor.

———

Bamberger's was, at that time, the great department store of the New Jersey region. It had just been bought by Macy's Store in New York and was in the process of getting adjusted to that exchange of ownership and its new slogan "It's Smart to be Thrifty."

I was assigned to the drapery department on the sixth floor. Mr. Edmunds was the floor manager and he did not know exactly what to do with me. He assigned me to the simple job of selling felt material in various colors which stood up in five foot rolls in one corner of the department while a cheerful little man, Mr. Weinberger, with a notable Brooklyn accent sold the drapery materials and mispronounced their French names.

I thought Mr. Weinberger was so badly educated that he probably couldn't do anything, but then I noticed that he sold twenty times as many draperies as I did. While I was scornful of Mr. Weinberger's language, I soon observed that he had a special gift. That gift was the gift of salesmanship. I realized it is a gift similar to writing fiction in the sense that the salesman has to believe in what he's selling just as the novelist must believe in his characters. Mr. Weinberger certainly believed. And he and the rest of the people in the drapery department made me acutely aware of how desperately people needed their jobs and what a fearful thing it would be if they lost them.

White felt was in much demand in September for parents to make into banners for their children's schools. I wanted to make as good an impression as I could for people needing my services, so I watched for them as they got off the sixth-floor escalator. I watched New Jersey housewives from Montclair and East Orange and all those other little towns. I would watch them get off the elevator looking around that large room toward the drapery department. I knew exactly what they would say as they approached me. When they saw my section they would say to me, "Where do I get felt?" It was almost impossible not to burst out laughing at that query although I did restrain myself from saying "Step right over." Sometimes they would stomp away to Mr. Edmunds and say, "What did that young man burst out laughing about? Did I say something funny?"

I took an apartment in East Orange on Mount Grove Street and took the street car to be at work at nine o'clock in the morning and work until five o'clock. It was, of course, hard work as we were not supposed to sit down on the job and we had our lunch at a hot dog cart near Bamberger's. It was a very rugged existence after all the comforts of college life with good food and not too much work to do.

My job at Bamberger's ended with the Christmas holidays, but Mother managed to get me a job on the copy desk at *Women's Wear Daily* which was run by the Fairchild family. So I went to work for *Women's Wear Daily* on 13th Street although I remained in East Orange. It took me at least two hours to get to work from East Orange on the Lackawanna and Hudson tubes, to Pennsylvania Station then across to Union Square.

The copy editor, my boss at *Women's Wear Daily,* was Sam Friedman, a wonderful-looking man who was a leader in the Communist Party and served as Norman Thomas's vice-presidential candidate. Sam was a patient man and taught me very quickly and easily the simple routines of the copy desk. It interested me partly because somehow I learned the names of all the state capitals throughout the United States and found that most useful all my life. Sam also let me do a little writing. I wrote the obituaries of deceased owners of women's dress stores that were phoned by the widows and I would take down their histories and prepare brief obituaries of those people.

Sam Friedman told me a lot about the wonders of Communism and I attended several Communist meetings with him which were in their main lecture hall in Union Square. It was a little hard for Sam to convince me much about Communists since I had been brought up by a family who worshiped Warren G. Harding and thought there was no politician as great as Warren G. Harding, whose political campaign had been performed from his porch in Marion, Ohio, which porch was much like ours in Newark. But I did get along fine with Sam. Of course it helped that he had a beautiful Russian wife.

During my several months at *Women's Wear,* I managed to learn useful things about the newspaper business. *Women's Wear Daily* ran two newspapers. *Women's Wear Daily* was for women's fashions and the *Daily News Record* covered the men's part of the dress business. So keeping their copy straight kept Sam Friedman and me fairly busy.

One dreary winter night in January 1931 I was taking notes for somebody's obituary. The phone rang and Sam Friedman handed it to me. It was Criss Brothers, the funeral company in Newark that had buried all the Spragues, telling me that my father had died that afternoon. While sweeping off the front porch he had collapsed in the living room with a massive heart failure. They wondered if I could get there the next morning on the night train, the St. Louisan from New York. Of course I had no money, but I remembered that I had the Frank and Giletti speakeasy's phone number. So I called and Frank answered. I told him that I needed money, fifty dollars to get on the St. Louisan that night at midnight from Pennsylvania Station. Sam said, "You get in a taxi and get up here, Marshall. I'll have the money for you." So I took a taxi to 46th Street where Frank and Giletti wished me well and commiserated with me for my loss.

I did make the train. The porter had no berth but let me sleep in the men's smoker. I was much too miserable and unhappy to drink any of the pint of applejack that Frank had given me.

I made it to Newark in the morning at the usual time and found Aunt Mary sad. She had arranged everything already. Dad was in his bed upstairs looking just as I had seen him in Princeton the year before. I sat with him holding his hand for half an hour and thinking of all the wonderful times the two of us had together. Criss Brothers had dressed him in one of Uncle Hal's hand-me-down fine London-tailored suits. Beside the couch where he loved to read *The Saturday Evening Post* on the ashtray was a note I had written him in Princeton promising that I would account for the $150 a month that I had asked him to give me my senior year, that I would list what I would spend it for. I would pay for all my clothes and keep out of debt. I thought of what a wonderful father he had been to me, how he had amused me and how he would break into profanity when he was with strangers to show them he was a regular guy. I remembered how much he had enjoyed the Hudson River Day Line expedition that time, even when the steamer pulled away before Mother had returned from the dock to buy aspirin. I remembered how he would exclaim, "Gad" when anything amazed him.

I remember that just before the funeral I said to him "Goodbye, Dad. Thanks for everything." Perhaps I added what he always said to me when I was little and he put me to bed, "Don't let the bedbugs bite."

We had the funeral in Aunt Mary's living room with the Reverend Franklin reading the Episcopal service. Of course, all the warehouse men from the store and Boom Brenner who had been manager for so many years were there and Aunt Mary and Grandma Osburn. That was all. Then we rode out to Cedar Hill and laid Dad to rest beside his father, Henry Day Sprague, who died in the 1890s, in the cemetery enclosure for which Uncle Hal had given Aunt Mary $5000 to shape up. So that was that.

Before I left, Aunt Mary, sad but inperturbable as ever, got $100 out of her safe in the front hall closet for me and my train fare, and $50 to pay back Frank and Giletti. I caught the train that same night and was able to be back at work on the copy desk with Sam Friedman the next morning.

Chapter Thirteen

MY PINK SLIP YEAR

MY ROMANCE with Edna Jane seemed to fade like the coming of twilight during the Depression years of 1930 and 1931. I was away from her all summer on the *Lancastria* cruise. When I returned in September I went to work at Bambergers. I had no time or energy. We did not write each other the kind of beautiful letters we wrote before, which so often sounded as if we were falling in love. EJ, of course, was preoccupied with graduating from Vassar in June of 1931, and I didn't seem to have the energy while I was working at Bamberger's or *Women's Wear* either. In any case, I missed our letters and discussions of Thomas Wolfe's *Look Homeward, Angel* and another book that I loved at that time, *A Tree Grows in Brooklyn*, by Betty Smith.

I knew, too, that EJ was worried about her father whose Wall Street brokerage business, like that of everyone in Wall Street, had not had an easy time through the Depression. At that time he was still sending EJ to Vassar and two sons to college. Just as I had decided to relieve Dad of supporting me, she wanted to help her father. She planned to take a course in shorthand and typing right after graduation aiming to get a job as soon as she could.

In the middle of March, Sam Friedman told me that he had to give me the pink slip much as he hated to do it. He said that Louis Fairchild had received complaints about the inaccuracy of some of my obits in which I had, out of sympathy for the bereaved widows, upgraded the standing of the deceased at the time of his death, raising him from a vice-president to a general manager, or even to a CEO.

Through Sam Friedman's kindness, I soon got another job at Fiction

House, publisher of pulpwood magazines which were the equivalent of today's television soap operas. Fiction House, like the main pulpwood publishers, Street and Smith, published several magazines like *Action Stories* and *Ranch Romances* and several others. They hired me as a reader. Of course, they were having a tough time making a go with the decline in circulation. My job was to take some of the old stories that were published years before in the magazine and rewrite the lead paragraphs, changing the names of the characters. Then they would reissue them as though they were new stories since they would not have to pay the authors the usual $50 any longer. They could fill the magazine with the revised old stories. We did get the authors' permission for the reissue, and they usually did not object to it as it at least kept their name alive as authors and the stories had no better use in the future anyhow. Some of the better authors of these pulpwood yarns included Wilkes Coburn, the Montana cowboy from Big Timber, and Eugene Cunningham, many of whose pulpwood stories ended up in grade-B cowboy movies.

After a couple of months working at Fiction House on the twenty-second floor of the News Building on 42nd Street near Grand Central Station, the magazine reduced its staff, and again I received a pink slip.

In mid-May of 1930 the department store business improved somewhat. As a result Bamberger's rehired some of the people they had let go after Christmas. I found myself assigned to the furniture department on the fifth floor.

In the meantime I was trying to write a short story or two to submit to Carl Brandt. I studied the stories in *The Saturday Evening Post* plotting them out paragraph by paragraph trying to learn how the authors made them readable and how they plotted them, although of course it is not possible to learn how to write fiction this way, and I do not recommend it.

One of my stories was called "George's Birthday" and I submitted it to Carl who sold it to a little magazine called *Mother's Home Weekly* for $25, of which Carl Brandt collected $2.50 as a commission for Brandt and Brandt.

Meanwhile, Mother's reporting on European fashions in Paris had been discontinued and she returned to 126 West 104th Street. One day Mother gave me a check for $700 that she had saved somehow, saying that she had never given me a graduation present and she knew I would like to have an automobile. The great car in the spring of 1931 was the

Model-A Ford which Henry Ford had created in 1928 replacing the old Model-T but with four-wheel brakes and standard shift and many other modern improvements. It was a very fine and most popular car.

So I went to the Theodore Luks Ford agency on West 57th Street and 12th Avenue and found a beautiful Model-A Ford convertible with canvas top. The salesman said that it had been sitting there for a couple of months because of the slow sales of cars at that time. I asked him if he would hold it until the next day when I would return and buy it. The salesman seemed very dubious. Where was I going to get the $679 that the car cost?

I went to Banker's Trust on 5th Avenue at 41st Street, cashed the $700 check. I folded the money carefully and put it in my shirt pocket, then started walking up 5th Avenue with my hand on that pocket watching to make sure nobody held me up or tried to get that money. I walked to 57th Street then crossed over from 5th Avenue to the Luks Agency beyond Carnegie Hall on 12th Avenue. I found my salesman. We sat down at a table as he gave me the instruction book which showed that my Model-A was a 24.6 horsepower car with a beautiful rumble seat, wire wheels, crank-up windows on both sides, a windshield wiper and a gray color that the instruction book called taupe. The salesman said dubiously, "How are you going to pay for it?" I took my hand off my pocket and pulled out the $700 and laid it on the table. The salesman said, "O my God." He picked up his phone and called the office on the sixth floor and said, "Send a guard down here. I've got a lot of money for him to take up to the safe." And so I paid for my first car and drove it away. I don't have to tell you that life has few more happy events. I give you the details of buying that Model-A because its career turned out to include practically all my life. I still have that car in my garage in Colorado as I write this.

I drove it up to Scarborough to show it to Edna Jane after her graduation in June. I remember that the two of us drove it along the beautiful Storm King Highway of the Palisades along the west side of the Hudson. We christened the Model-A and Edna Jane named it Calliope because it was so noisy. That was shortened in time by our children from Calliope, which they could not pronounce, to Cloppy.

———

I was busy working in the furniture department of Bamberger's. Meanwhile EJ got a job in New York on the Sunday Suburban section of *The*

New York Times to try the shorthand she had learned before in Yonkers. I saw her only a few times during that summer and fall and even into the winter. In all that time when I always thought of her as my girl, we did not discuss marriage which, of course, would have been useless because nobody could afford marriage during those depression days with salaries as low as $6 a week. Both of us put it out of our minds as something not to be considered for many months to come.

In the spring of 1932 I took the week off from Bamberger's. My Princeton roommate, Chick Shenk, came to East Orange from his home in Erie, Pennsylvania. The two of us rode in the Model-A to the wedding of a classmate friend in Waterbury, Connecticut, where we scooped up the free champagne. After the wedding and feeling no pain, Chick suggested we stop in Scarborough and see if Edna Jane happened to be there that weekend. So we did. There was nobody home in Scarborough except my old friend Bin the three hundred pound black cook who had been so good to me in the days when I was visiting Sallie Ailes so often. I asked Bin about Edna Jane. We had sat down for coffee, and Bin suddenly looked very solemn. Then she said, "When the cat's away, the mice will play." I wondered all the way to East Orange what she had meant. In East Orange there was a letter for me from Sallie Ailes. It was an invitation to Edna Jane's wedding in Scarborough on June 4th, 1932.

Chapter Fourteen

WHERE THERE'S A WILL

THE LOSS of my best girl was bad enough. A few days later the manager at the furniture department of Bamberger's gave me my fourth pink slip. When I went to get my separation pay, the girl at the cashier's desk looked at my sorrowful face and burst into tears. Of course, with no job I had to give up paying my share of the East Orange apartment I shared with Frank Chase. I moved to Mother's large studio on 104th Street.

I moped my way through the summer heat. I wrote a couple of stories for Carl Brandt which were promptly rejected by *The Saturday Evening Post* with the kindly notes that editors always send urging me to keep trying.

When I told Hugh Kahler about the rejection slips, he and his wife tried to cheer me up. They told me to give the Model-A a trial run and go to Kennebunkport, Maine, to meet his old friend and neighbor Booth Tarkington. I talked to Booth Tarkington about writing and asked him how I could learn to write. He said, "Nobody can teach you how to write. You learn by writing because there's nothing else you want to do. Don't worry about rejection slips. I collected a bushel basket of them before—after ten years of trying—a publisher in 1900 took a chance on my novel *Monsieur Beaucaire*. It's still selling quite well after thirty years." Mr. Tarkington, at the age of seventy, was dictating his new novel, *Presenting Lily Mars,* to his secretary Betty Trotter because he was almost totally blind.

Mother, meanwhile, did not know what to do with me through that summer into the fall and wrote Josie of my jobless despair. Josie and Howard Taylor had been transferred from Hamburg to Tientsin, China, where he was in charge of imports to North China. In a few weeks Josie wrote me that the Depression had not been felt in North China as yet and if I would come to Tientsin, which was the treaty port of Peking, that she was sure that I could get a job.

I told Carl Brandt of Josie's suggestion, adding that I would not mind going to China but I didn't have the money to get there. Carl replied, "Didn't you tell me that your brother-in-law was in the American consulate in Tientsin? He must have something to do with the import of oil and gasoline. Why don't you go down to the Standard Oil Company in New York and ask them to give you a ride to China on one of their tankers out of California?"

I went down to the Bowery and was directed to the office of the Socony Vacuum Company which delivered much of the oil and gasoline to North China. Socony Vacuum seemed interested in my request. The manager said, "I think we can arrange that." Later in the fall he told me that one of their leased Norwegian oil tankers called the *Hallanger* was sailing from San Pedro, California, to Tientsin on February 4, 1933. The captain's name was Johann Abrahamson, who said he and his two mates on the ship would be glad to have me to practice their English and maybe I could teach him how to play bridge. I told Carl Brandt that I had my trip to China, but I didn't have enough money to get myself to San Pedro, California. Again I reminded Carl that I was broke and he said, "I thought of that. Can you get $25 to get yourself to Montreal? One of my writers there is editor of *The Canadian National Railways Magazine*. He said he can give you a pass on one of his trains for the four thousand miles across Canada to Vancouver."

Late in January of 1933, Mother saw me off from Grand Central Station to Montreal. From there I soon found myself with my pass on a Pullman car heading west on Canadian National Railways for Vancouver. That railway ran in a route north of the more popular Canadian Pacific. My cheerful Pullman porter took very good care of me because I was the only passenger on the run. After a day in Vancouver I got on a bus and rode to Seattle, Portland and western Oregon. I spent a night in San Francisco, then down to Los Angeles and San Pedro which was the main distribution point for shipping oil and gasoline to consumers in Asia.

I was delighted to leave the winter of Vancouver behind me and find myself in the spring-like weather of Los Angeles, though I noted in particular once more the seriousness of the Depression as cafes in Los Angeles had signs in their windows urging me to have breakfast of bacon and eggs, toast and orange juice for fifteen cents.

A few miles south of Los Angeles in San Pedro I found my tanker the *Hallanger*. I thought that it was a frightful white monster, rising fifty feet above the harbor and with a smiling prow looked as though it would like to bite me. I found the *Hallanger's* captain, Johann Abrahamson. He was a genial 240-pound man who spoke broken English. He led me down the ninety-foot catwalk of the tanker to his lordly quarters in front and showed me his stateroom below the tanker's bridge and chart room, then to his quarters which were so neat and comfortable. My stateroom adjoined his and was very pleasant, about eight-by-forty-feet wide with a comfortable bunk, a desk, two large windows and a tile bathroom. Very elegant setup.

Captain Abrahamson told me that the *Hallanger* was a diesel motor ship that moved about ten knots an hour in calm weather. The twelve-cylinder engine was much like an automobile engine in principle, but ran on crude oil rather than gasoline. The engine was operated by ten sailors. The tanker was 493 feet long with a dead weight of 13,500 tons carrying 12,000 tons of gasoline, kerosene and oil in ten tanks separated by bulkheads with valves greased daily by twelve of the deckhands. The *Hallanger* seemed huge to me but was tiny compared to those 100,000 ton tankers that carry oil out of the Persian Gulf to the United States.

The captain told me that the crew totaled thirty-four men, aged sixteen to forty-eight, mostly natives of Bergen, Norway. They included a cook, assistant cook and mess hand. Besides the captain, the ship had a chief officer and a first and second mate with living quarters under the chart room below the captain's quarters.

The mates took their meals with the crew in back and not in the captain's elegant salon. Our meals, I learned, were served to us from the kitchen in the crew's quarters in the prow of the boat by a steward whose name was Einar Hillands. He would carry our meals from the kitchen along the hundred-yard plank to the captain's quarters, carrying them overhead and balancing with the gentle roll of the boat on a special warming tray.

So on the 4th of February, 1933, at 8 A.M., we moved out of San Pedro harbor past several vessels of the U.S. Naval fleet.

Chapter Fifteen

ON A SLOW BOAT TO CHINA

ON A MOST beautiful day we moved away from the coast past Catalina Island and on a bit north for an hour or so and veered a little to the south to reach the 30th Parallel along which we would sail for eight thousand miles to the southern tip of Japan passing eighty miles north of Honolulu and two hundred miles north of Midway Island, the captain said. New Orleans, you may remember, is on the 30th Parallel, so we could expect similar weather on our trip. At the southern tip of Japan, the province of Kyushu, we would travel into the East China Sea where we would leave the 30th Parallel and move along the west coast of Japan, around Korea, and into the Yellow Sea to Taku Bay, the little port of Tientsin on the 39th Parallel. The bay is so shallow that the tanker would not be able to get closer than twelve miles to the port. From there the gasoline would have to be hauled from the tanker to Tientsin.

As we left San Pedro on the *Hallanger,* I began to wonder if I would starve to death on the thirty-day, eight thousand-mile passage to Tientsin. I did not need to worry. Here's a listing of what Captain Abrahamson, the thirty-four members of the crew and I put away every day. Starting promptly at 7:30 every morning the slight, sandy-haired Einar Hilland walked the hundred-yard gangplank catwalk from the kitchen in the rear with a tray of rolls and hot coffee for the Captain and me. At 9:00 A.M. Einar carried a larger tray for breakfast of grapefruit, corn flakes (provided especially for me, I was told), eggs, ham, baked beans, toast, jam, cheese and more hot coffee. At 12:30 P.M. came the day's main meal, soup, roast chicken, roast beef, boiled potatoes with gravy, fresh sliced oranges or pears or boiled apples for dessert, all washed down with a jigger of Swedish aqua vitae, the cordial of the Norwegians.

We got nothing more to eat until 3:00 P.M. when Einar brought us coffee and cookies. Supper at 7:00 P.M. was a sort of buffet to sustain us through the night. It consisted of five different sliced meats on five saucers, liver sausage, horse sausage, cold ham, brain cheese, a bowl of salad and slices of bread and a pot of jam. Then the main dish, halibut or salmon. No dessert, thank God for that.

Later the steward showed me in the back part of the tanker, in the crew's quarters, how the food supplies were stored in a huge and spotless storeroom with dozens of shelves that resembled in its variety the inside of Safeway stores. Near the storeroom was an enormous refrigerator with bacon and eggs, fresh vegetables and fruits. All these perishables, the captain told me, were replaced at the end of the ship's thirty-day run between North China and San Pedro, California. Incidentally, on its return from North China the *Hallanger* ran eastward on the 40th Parallel because the winds were more favorable.

Perhaps you wonder how I passed all those twenty-nine days on the Pacific, isolated as I was with the captain in my comfortable little cabin. I don't think that Abrahamson learned much bridge from me since I didn't know how to bid in Norwegian. I never did learn how to say "Three No Trump." In rainy weather, which wasn't very often, I typed notes of what I saw. I took a few hours to write a short story which was called "Drawing Room A" for the *Canadian National Railways Magazine*. It was kind of a silly story, but they published it anyway.

I spent many hours on the bridge with the first and second mates. Sometimes I even steered that 12,000-ton tanker, which was probably forbidden. One of these mates was an old-timer from the tramp-steamer days. He had been to every port in the world.

Of course, I studied the sea birds, especially the California pilot birds that were always in our wake. They moved fast but I never saw their wings flap as they just had a trick of gliding with the air currents.

I stayed up many nights on the bridge studying the stars. I had my star book along. There couldn't have been a more perfect place to see the stars because the whole sky was there before me to the horizon. I learned the position of Procyon, Canopus, Capella, Aldebaran, Betelgeuse, and studied Castor and Pollux, Regulus, Polaris, the planets Venus and Jupiter. It was a fascinating thing because there were stars on the 30th Parallel which I never saw or would see again, such as the beautiful Southern Cross that I had heard about but never seen.

Some fascinating thing would happen almost every day, like the day I saw a flying fish landing on the deck. I caught it, a pretty little fish about nine inches long. I took it, cleaned it like a Maine brook trout, had the cook fry it in butter for supper. It tasted very good, very fresh, of course.

We never saw any other boats practically the whole run. I guess our route on the 30th Parallel was not a very popular one. But on February 23, the nineteenth day out, as we were heading for Japan, as Captain Abrahamson and I were preparing to skip a day at the International Date Line, suddenly a small ship about eighty feet long chugged into view with three or four of its crew watching us. We were then one thousand miles from the southern tip of Japan. The ship was marked with yellow streaks, dagger-shaped. The captain told me it was a Japanese fishing boat much farther from shore than they usually were.

The dozen men of the crew waved wildly at us and pointed at a huge fish hoisted in plain view. The captain stopped the tanker's motor and then started it which caused consternation on the fishing boat. It hoisted what the captain said was a distress signal. The captain stopped the engines of the tanker again as the fishing boat approached on the lee side of the gently rolling tanker. I learned later that it cost a lot of money to stop a tanker. When the fishing boat was about twenty yards away, one of the Japanese sailors jumped into the warm water and paddled his way to us. He swam along side the tanker to grab the rope ladder that the captain put down. He caught the rope ladder on the roll of the ship and once on deck nodded proudly at me and made signs to the captain that indicated that the fishing boat had lost its way. The captain sent him to the chart room to determine his position.

He told me that the Japanese did not even carry a compass. In this case the boat, if it had headed west from where we were, would have missed Japan entirely and gone all the way to China instead of its real destination which was probably Yokohama. The captain said that the Japanese were not very good sailors for a sea-bound country and did not take too much interest in the sea except enough to get fish for food.

While I was watching the little ship and the Japanese that came aboard, I had one of those nutty impulses that everyone has now and then. I had no idea if there were any man-eating sharks in this part of the tranquil, blue Pacific and figured that if so they would have eaten the Japanese sailor if they were hungry. So I stripped down to my shorts and dove the thirty or forty feet from the tanker's deck into the Pacific. The water was pleasantly warm and though I looked around a little bit for sharks I didn't see any. I thought, meanwhile, what a damn fool I was, but how much fun it was to swim a thousand miles from land with all the crew hanging on to the edge of the tanker watching me with astonishment. But I miscalculated one thing about this swim. The tanker was rolling gently and the rope ladder had risen 30 feet above the water, so I had to wait interminably until the tanker rolled the other way and the ladder came within my reach. Then I grabbed it and climbed aboard, feeling glad to be back.

Meanwhile the Japanese hoisted the 35-pound sturgeon they had caught that morning and gave it to us in gratitude for stopping and showing them the charts. All of us, crew, captain and everyone ate it and found it to be delicious. It tasted a little like veal. The captain had given the Japanese sailor a map with the route marked on it to Yoko-hama and a bottle of aqua vitae as a goodwill gesture to Japan. The captain told me later that the cost of stopping the tanker's motors for an hour was about $30. He went on to explain that when ships break down and have to be towed to port for repair, it is understood that the boat doing the towing would receive a third of the registered value of the towed boat. This sum is divided two-thirds to the tow ship's owners and one-third to the crew. This probably explains why ships are so eager to rush to the rescue of ships in trouble.

On February 27, 1933, about our 23rd day out of San Pedro, we spotted Torre Shima, a tiny island 470 miles from Tanega Shima, at the southern tip of Japan. We passed through Tanega Strait on March 1st and began heading northward past Nagasaki and around Quelque Pari Island at the southern tip and coasted along the beautiful west coast of Japan and then a day or two later around Korea. The next day or two it was getting noticeably colder than that beautiful summer sunshine we had known for so long as we now moved back into winter in the north where Tientsin was. I should repeat how beautiful that west side of Japan looked as we passed not too far away. Looking at the little rising part of the coast made me realize why the Japanese who have so much beauty close up are so eager to have beauty in their lives.

As the captain and I began piling on warmer clothes, the tanker swung around the Shantung promontory of China and into the Gulf of Chihla some five hundred miles from Taku. On March 4th the tanker's radio operator sent a message to my sister, Josie Taylor, in Tientsin to tell her we expected to arrive the next day. On March 5th the whole front of the tanker wore a thick coating of ice. We passed Port Arthur at noon where the Japanese had battled the Russians in 1904. Chihla Bay is so shallow that we could not get any closer to Taku than 12 miles. Captain Abrahamson had his crew on the prow, taking soundings, and when they measured eighteen feet he dropped anchor.

Meanwhile, from Taku a tug appeared pulling a lighter. The captain began pumping gasoline into the lighter for delivery to Tientsin. He told me that the remaining gasoline in the tanker would be delivered to Dairien in Manchuria, to be used by the Japanese army to move south from Manchuria through the province of Jehol to occupy north China.

While the lighter was being loaded with gasoline for Tientsin, I said goodbye to my good friends on the *Hallanger* and with my typewriter and suitcase I climbed aboard the small coal-fired Chinese tug that would tow the lighter from Taku Bar thirty miles up the Peitaho River to the British concession adjoining Tientsin. I spent a cold miserable two nights in the cabin of that tug with nothing to eat but a bowl of rice and some funny tasting fish. There was a young Englishman on the tug with me, and a Eurasian, part Chinese and part Portuguese, who worked for Socony Vacuum. They told me that the word "Tientsin" meant "heaven ford" in English. I had hoped that they would tell me something about Tientsin and the British concession, but all they would talk about was the current badminton tournament at the Tientsin Country Club.

Perhaps I had had more horrible nights than those nights on that tug, but if so I can't remember. The river had a thin coating of ice, and there was a great racket of the tug breaking through the ice. The Englishman told me that he had heard rumors that the Japanese might capture the lighter at Taku Bar to get the gasoline. They had already seized the whole of Manchuria and were preparing to seize the next province south, Jehol, before capturing the whole of North China.

The tug and the lighter got through to the British concession at dawn and dropped the lighter at Gutterson and Swirg's go-down. There I could see a tall man in a tuxedo on the Tientsin bund, waving. This was Howard Taylor, called Howie. Beside him was a tall Chinese in a white jacket and pants, Howie's number one boy, Khan. Howie was in evening dress because he and Josie had given a party at their home at 19 Bureau Street to welcome me to Tientsin and China.

Chapter Sixteen

Tientsin—"Heaven Ford"

K HAN, HOWIE'S NUMBER one boy, took my suitcase and Remington typewriter with a fold-in keyboard and pushed me up the slope of the bund to be welcomed by Howie. He said that Josie had had a party that night to greet me, but she had sent the guests home when she learned that the tug would not arrive until 4:00 A.M.

Howie said, "This is Victoria Road." I glanced down the street and saw a large store with a man sleeping on the pavement at the entrance. I asked Howie what that man was doing there. Howie said, "Oh, he's guarding the store. It is cheaper in China to have a man sleep outside the store door even in the dead of winter than to pay for burglary insurance."

Then I noticed that Howie had a Colt pistol in a holster around his waist. I said, "What's that gun for, Howie?" He replied, "We expect the Japanese to come down from Manchuria through Jehol to occupy North China soon."

We walked on a block or two to the townhouse where Howie and Josie lived. I began to revive somewhat in anticipation of seeing Josie and meeting her infant son Erik who had been born in Tientsin two years before. When we walked up the stairs to go into the townhouse, a rickshaw pulled up next door with two ladies dressed in evening dress. They were, Howie said, Russian hostesses for a nightclub in the French Concession coming home from work at dawn.

We walked into the living room of the townhouse. In the light of dawn the first thing I spotted was Mother's Steinway piano which the consular service had shipped ten thousand miles from New York to

Germany and on to China. A table stood in the living room all set up. The Taylor's Chinese cook came in and asked me in English what I wanted for breakfast. I said, "Bacon and eggs." Howie said, "Give him some of those corn flakes I bought yesterday."

Then three other people appeared and stood by the cook watching me as though I were a strange wild animal. With them was a young man my age who, Howie said, was his "number two" boy who did chores around the house. The other two were tiny women with bound feet. One of the women, Howie said, was Erik's amah or nurse. The other woman was the family's "sew-sew" amah who worked full-time mending clothes and ironing handkerchiefs and so on.

After my delightful 4 A.M. American breakfast I went upstairs and got out of my soot-stained clothes and gratefully went to bed. When I woke up later in the morning, I found my clothes and my shoes had been picked up by the number two boy who cleaned and pressed the suit and shined the shoes. So this was China, I thought. What a wonderful place! I was beginning to like China.

I felt refreshed. After a bath, I put on my clean clothes and ordered another American breakfast of bacon and eggs.

I was happy when Josie, looking healthy, joined us at breakfast. The amah carried in the baby, Erik, who chattered away in Chinese that he had picked up from his amah.

I told Josie how much I admired the breakfasts her cook had served me. "Oh," Josie said, "I hired him away from the best restaurant in Peking, the Grand Hotel des Wagonlits where all the diplomats dine. I was pleased to get such a fine cook. Last month I found that he charges me the same price for each of our meals as is charged at the high-priced Grand Hotel restaurant in Peiping."

I had left New York in such a rush that I did not have time to find out anything about China and its history. I remembered that Miss Beecher had told my third grade class in Newark that China had a population of about a billion people. Howie Taylor had done a lot of reading about China and began telling me about Tientsin. He said Tientsin with 3,000,000 people was the second largest city in China after Shanghai which had a population of 3,500,000 people. Peiping had a population of 2,500,000, and Hong Kong was the other large city with 2,300,000 people.

He explained how after the Opium War of 1842 with England, a group of English shippers including Jardine Matthesson had leased from China for ninety-nine years a large beautiful harbor that became the city of Hong Kong. They overcame the difficulty of the Chinese language and its many dialects by developing a corps of English-speaking Chinese who did their business in China for them. These were called "compradores," as they still were in 1933.

The English did so well in Hong Kong that they along with French and other Europeans moved on seven hundred miles into North China, which they found equally profitable. In fact the profit was so great in 1900 that a cult of militant Chinese became envious and decided to drive the foreigners out. This group called themselves "The Society of Harmonious Fists," hence the foreigners came to give them the name "Boxers." In June of 1900, the Boxers laid siege to all foreigners in Tientsin and Peiping, ninety miles away. They destroyed many businesses, embassies, legations and missions and murdered every European they could find, a total of 291. The murderous siege lasted thirty-nine days. The Europeans responded to the slaughter by calling in military units.

The Boxer tragedy occurred while China was ruled by the dowager empress of the Manchu dynasty which had ruled China for many centuries. Howie said that at the height of the Manchu power Peking was described by historians as the most lavish and glittering capital in the world, even more beautiful than Paris of Louis XIV. In later years the rule of the dowager empress in Peking was greatly weakened by the corrupt, militant war lords who controlled various provinces on her behalf.

For some years beginning in 1908, the empress compensated England and France and other foreign traders in Tientsin for their losses in the Boxer rebellion. She gave the foreigners farm-sized acreages of land along the Hai Ho River adjoining the large city of Tientsin. These acreages along the river were called concessions. They were given to the British, the Italians, the Germans, the French, the Russians and the Japanese. The wealthiest of these was the British Concession with a population of about five thousand. The United States had a concession for a time. The concessions were not subject to Chinese jurisdictions of any kind. Elected councilors had complete charge of all affairs in each concession, including courts, utilities, police departments, collection of taxes, street departments, etc.

The U.S. Concession in the area where Howie and Josie Taylor lived was returned to the Chinese. The German Concession went back after World War I as dictated by the Versailles Treaty.

In 1911 the ancient kingdom of the Manchu dynasty and its aging dowager empress was overthrown with the aid of China's national hero Sun Yat-sen who founded the Kuomintang or National People's Party. Sun Yat-sen died in 1926 and was replaced as head of the party by Chiang Kai-Shek who unified the country with the support of the Russian Communists and the Japanese.

Howie went on to explain that North China and its concessions in Tientsin became thereafter very popular with businessmen and diplomats because Chinese currency had been so depreciated that living there was very cheap. One American dollar was worth twenty Chinese dollars (yuans) which, in effect, made living costs in China one-twentieth of what they would have been in the United States. This was why Howie and Josie could afford five full-time servants and their townhouse on Biever Street.

After briefing me on Chinese history, Howie went on to tell me that he had found a job for me as a reporter on the *North China Star* whose reporter had left Tientsin to take a job with Reuters News Service in Singapore. Of course, that was the kind of job I had wanted for years.

Howie then took me in a rickshaw down Victoria Road to meet Charles James Fox, the editor of the *North China Star* on Rue Pasteur in the French Concession. The two of us met Mr. Fox in the news room of the paper on the second floor. Mr. Fox was a portly gentleman smelling pleasantly of bourbon of which, Howie said, he was very fond.

According to Howie Charles James Fox had been a newspaperman in Baltimore and had been Maryland manager of Theodore Roosevelt's 1912 Bull Moose campaign to win the presidency from the Democrat Woodrow Wilson. Fox was so despondent when Roosevelt lost that he sold his home in Baltimore and went as far away from the United States as he could get—to Tientsin, China. He found that Tientsin had only one daily paper, *The Peking and Tientsin Times,* to serve the ten thousand residents of the foreign concessions. So he decided to start an American paper for the members of the Fifteenth U.S. Infantry stationed there to protect American property, and for employees of various American businesses and of the American Consulate General where Howie worked.

On April 13, 1933, at 2:00 P.M. I arrived at 77 Rue Pasteur as directed by Mr. Fox and took my seat at the news desk on the second floor of the *North China Star* opposite Carlos Da Costa, my news editor. Mr. Da Costa greeted me warmly and apologized for yawning saying he had spent half the night playing Mahjong in the native city with his friends. He went on to explain that my hours would be from 2:00 P.M. to 10:00 at night or whenever it was time to put the paper to bed. He said he filled the paper with Associated Press wire news and with boiler plates and photo plates from United Press.

My job would be to fill in with local stories as I came across them. He said I would routinely call each day to Mayford Barrett who was press officer at the Fifteenth U.S. Infantry. I would go on to the American Consulate General for any news that might have developed there that would be given me by the senior consul, Angus Ward, under the Consul General, Frank Lockhart. From the Consul General I would proceed to the British Concession City Hall for news from the Russian chief of police Mr. Soukaroff. Next Carlos told me that my rickshaw would take me to the Fifteenth U.S. Infantry if I told him to go to Wobbay Ming Ching Pao which was Chinese for the Fifteenth U.S. Infantry. The words to get my rickshaw to the Consulate General were "Megwa Lang Pao" which was Chinese for the American Consulate.

Carlos Da Costa assured me that he would leave the choice of local stories up to me without asking him. I was pleased that I had the responsibility of picking my own stories to write for Carlos. I probably should have been appalled, but when I wrote for *The Lit* at Lawrenceville I had to decide what would interest my readers at that time. So I decided I would use the same system in judging what was worth writing about for readers in the Concessions.

My first story was a feature story about the popular Victoria Park across the street from Antlers House Hotel where the amahs took the children. So I listened to their chatter a moment or two. I told how one child picked up a stone and gave it to her solemn amah who took the stone, put it in her mouth and swallowed it.

Carlos told me not to mind Angus Ward's gruffness at the American Consulate. He did not care much for newspapermen, and had a couple of dogs at his house to keep them at bay. He added that Angus had completed a dictionary of the Mongolian language and would probably be transferred to Moscow soon as he was interested in the development of the Communist Party there.

Carlos said that at City Hall I would enjoy an American from Baltimore named Calvin Joyner who was in charge of the British Concession utilities. Joyner made a hobby of telescopes which he used to study the planet Mars which interested him because he knew that someday the Americans would find a way to travel in space.

I had been on my newspaper job less than a week when my brother-in-law Howie Taylor was called to Washington by the consular service to report on rumors of the Japanese plan to invade North China and seize all property in Tientsin and Peking. Howie and Josie closed their house on Biever Street, dismissed the five servants, packed up the Steinway and arranged to sail from Kobe, Japan, on the Silver Dollar steamer *President Wilson,* planning to send Josie and Erik on from San Francisco to Howie's parents in Vermillion, South Dakota, to show them their grandson Erik. Before Josie and Howie left Tientsin for the United States, he arranged for me to stay at the Talati House Hotel on Victoria Road where I had a comfortable room.

Chapter Seventeen

THE CHINA HAND

L OOKING OVER the clipping book of hundreds of stories I wrote during my year as a reporter for the *North China Star* starting in April 1933, I am astonished by the activities of the residents of the four foreign concessions of Tientsin in their clubs, sports events, social events, military ceremonials for the leaders of their various countries, holidays, church affairs such as the large well-attended rummage sale at All Saints Episcopal Church and its annual Crib Banquet to collect funds for needy children. I wondered how any of the residents had any time to sleep. The underlying reason was homesickness. They tried to carry on in their concessions the same sort of activities that they had known back home.

Of course, there were hundreds of clubs maintained within each concession. They all had lavish annual dinners which required mention in the *North China Star*.

Then there were the meets of the Tientsin Hunt Clubs which ran a steeplechase and also used their horses for the races at Tientsin Race Club with "Gentlemen Riders" mostly from the Tientsin Country Club. In the summer there were polo games on Dumbarton Field near the Country Club attended by people watching the polo from their cars.

I wrote about how the commander of the Fifteenth U.S. Infantry Karl Truesdell and two of his aides went to Peking where they hired a bull to haul their wagon of hunting supplies and went on an eighteen-day hunting trip a hundred miles west of Peking in the mountains of

Inner Mongolia which they found filled with all kinds of game. The hunters made their headquarters in the Catholic mission of Kouyang. It was a most successful hunt. They returned with three mountain sheep which Colonel Truesdell told me were Ovis Carli. They also saw many birds like the very large Chinese bustards, and grouse like American grouse which gave them their food on the trip. They did shoot a couple of roebucks.

———

In June I wrote many stories about the Tientsin residents' difficulties getting away from the horrible heat to Taku Bay and from there to the resort town of Peita Ho Beach where there was a cabin colony on the beach. The year of 1933 was a difficult time to get to the beach because of the fear of Japanese invasion. There were Japanese soldiers stopping the railroads all the time. Sometimes people from Tientsin would go by train down to Taku Bar and take small steamers from there for the eighteen-hour sail to Peita Ho, but the trains were seldom on time and it was difficult to get passage on the small boat from Chung King to Peita Ho at Ching Wang Tao. It usually took a couple of days for the wives to make it to Peita Ho with their children and their amahs and beach equipment and always with interruptions along the way.

I had fun writing fake letters to the editor as newspaper staffers often do when not enough letters come in. I wrote one signed Medford Twinkle. It had to do with a story we had run from Australia which had kangaroos in trees. Medford Twinkle said, "That's impossible. They don't know how to climb trees!"

I was especially pleased when the British invited me to a gala dinner in celebration of King George's birthday during which we sang "Do Ye Ken, John Peel" and "Auld Lang Syne." After that nice English dinner I became a fervent admirer of the British and their ways, though I still preferred to be an American.

At Easter time I covered children's egg hunts in most of the concessions. Even the Japanese had an egg hunt.

I made a trip or two into the huge Chinese city to visit one of the paintbrush factories. Tientsin was a center for making hog bristle paint brushes which were in great demand in the United States. Other Tientsin industries were mills for silk and cotton products.

Occasional gasoline wars occurred between the gas companies with offices in Tientsin like the Texas Company, Socony Vacuum, Standard Oil of New Jersey, British Petroleum, the United Petroleum Trust of Soviet Russia and the Tahwa Petroleum Company, a Chinese company. Between the wars the price of gasoline might range from fifty cents a gallon to as much as seventy cents a gallon which, of course, outraged all the foreigners in the concessions.

On my day off my friend Jerry Warner, a Consul, and I usually went to the Golden Ship Night Club in the French Concession. The Club had a juke box for dancing with their Japanese hostesses, although they only had a couple of Louis Armstrong records. One of them was "West Side Blues" which had a marvelous piano solo by Earl Hines.

Ed Eicholholzer, the Standard Oil manager for Tientsin, invited me to make a sales trip in the company's 1925 Dodge southward a couple hundred miles, much of it along the Yellow River to a small village where we spent the night in a hut with isinglass windows and were serenaded by a Chinese flute player playing twelve-tone melodies.

In the morning I took a walk by myself to look at a war lord's fort not too far from the village. As I watched the fort from a hundred yards, I saw a sentry come out with a long rifle. I turned around and went back to the village. The comprador who had accompanied us on this kerosene sales trip told me he had sent word to the war lord that a young American might approach the fort but that he was harmless. The war lord had an American named Bert Hall in his jail who had told the comprador he was there because he had been paid $9000 to deliver machine guns to the war lord, but he had never delivered the guns.

I wrote a story about a brief visit south of Tientsin to the western tombs where several centuries of Manchu dynasty rulers were buried. There was an automobile road from Tientsin eighty-five miles to Peking, but it was a brave driver who attempted to get there on it. It was filled with deep ditches dug by the Chinese to impede travel if the Japanese invaded.

I had fun writing an article about three pretty girls from Bartlesville, Oklahoma, Brownsville, Texas, and Buffalo, New York, who showed up in the British Concession sent by *Time* to sell magazine subscriptions. Since there no jobs at home, they had got the circulation department of the magazine to send them around the world. They continued their adventurous trip eastward to Singapore through the Suez Canal across the Mediterranean to New York and home again.

Of course, I covered the lavish wedding of Winnie Tipper to Leo Thomas in All Saints Church. The wedding was as elaborate as any royal wedding in Westminster Abbey as the two were both members of pioneer families who had been in Tientsin almost from the beginning.

I wrote a story about a party given by a dozen American bachelors including me, for which Carlos Da Costa wrote a headline "American Bachelors Give Blowout at West Lake Hotel."

I barely survived the glut of stories about Christmas festivities in the four concessions, doing my bit on the *North China Star* for Christmas cheer. I wrote a story urging children to believe in Santa Claus. It was about a father who told his children it was all nonsense until a child found a twenty-dollar bill under the bed and gave it to the father. He immediately changed his mind and said he did believe in Santa after all.

I covered an event created by a department store that hired a plane in Shanghai to bring Santa Claus with a lot of children's toys to land on the Army's Can-Do field. About two thousand children assembled for that thrilling event and watched Santa jump out of the plane and begin distributing toys.

I also wrote a Christmas poem in imitation of the poem Frank Sullivan wrote each year in *The New Yorker*. Carlos Da Costa ran it on the front page. My poem read:

> 'Twas the night before Christmas and all through the Town
> Was the hustle and bustle of Men of Renown
> Getting dressed with Decorum in every abode
> For a glittering trip down Victoria Road,
> With manicured Fingers and neatly combed Hair,
> Their Silk hats a-gleam in the cold Winter air.
>
> The Customs Commissioner, the Brigadier,
> Municipal Chairmen and Councilmen dear
> Heads of the Rotary, Legion and Shriners,
> Lions and War Vets and K.M.A. Miners,
> C-G's and Colonels, impatient to go forth,

Consuls and Majors, Police Chiefs and so forth.
For Tientsin Officials without an exception
Were asked to attend the Official Reception
Of good old St. Nicholas, Statesmen Ephemeral,
  Held at the big Christmas Consulate General.
There was no whispered comment, no treading on toes,
International jealousies never arose;
The issue of Christmas 'twas easy to see,
Every delegate present was bound to agree.

And so I went on to conclude this horrible poem.

During that year of 1933, I wrote endless stories of baseball games played between the U.S. Army and the Japanese on three fields. And football games. And winter boxing fights in the recreation room. If facilities didn't exist for a sport, they built one. The English dammed up a mile of the trickling Hai Ho River to form a mile-long lake so that former members of the Oxford crew could have a regatta. The U.S. Army had some hockey players, so on a twenty-degree-below-zero month they rimmed with boards a football-field-sized flat space and flooded it to make a hockey rink which they covered with tarps and claimed the biggest in the world. The golfers at the country club built a nine-hole golf course with sand greens and traps near the club on an inhospitable prairie. As Howie said, "That course consisted entirely of sand traps."

I even managed to write a story about a men's beauty contest which was won by Captain Federico Martinengo. He was a tall, handsome man with the ineffable attraction for women that so many Italian men have. All the women in the British Concession swooned over Federico, but he never allowed himself to get involved with any of them. I noticed that he kept his physique because he never stayed at parties past 11:00 P.M. which was his way of preserving his virility, he said.

I did endure the all-night full dress New Year's Eve at the Tientsin Country Club which was very much like New Year's Eve in the United States in its uninhibited nonsense and the uninhibited determination of the Tientsiners to be gay and fascinating.

I had things to cover that were not so much fun such as the arrival on the north side of Tientsin of ten thousand refugees fleeing ahead of the Japanese army approaching from Manchuria through Jehol. These

Chinese farmers showed great ingenuity in setting up their refugee camps with women on one side of their straw-filled compounds and men on the other. Everything was very orderly.

I covered an explosion in the east railroad station. I hurried down there just after someone had thrown a bomb into a train thinking Russians might be on it. It had killed several coolies.

I had fun with one long story which was given me by a sergeant about the personalities of his army mules of which he was very fond.

January of 1934 was a miserable month in Tientsin, cold and some snow. I came down with the flu in my room at the Talati House. I was getting quite bored with the Talati Restaurant although Mr. Talati tried to vary the flavor of his curry with an amazing variety of different meats, including what I suspected was horse meat. His condiments were always interesting, varieties of chutney, onion, coconut, bits of hard-boiled egg, peanuts, candied ginger and assorted spices.

To tell the truth, I was beginning to get tired of the long stories I had to write for the *North China Star* about nothing of any special importance. Also I yearned often for a chocolate malted milk shake and a musical comedy like "Girl Crazy." I had begun to realize that I could not afford the passage from Kobe, Japan, on the very expensive ships to San Francisco with the further cost of rail passage to New York.

Early in March of 1934, Dr. H. Betz, the German Consul General in Tientsin returned from a vacation in Berlin after a twelve-day ride on the trans-Siberian Railroad to Harbin and Mukden. Carlos Da Costa asked me to interview him. The Consul General was a nervous little man with a thick German accent, but I was interested in his description of conditions in Germany under Adolf Hitler. He became quite heated discussing what he termed "outrageous lies" in the American papers about the persecution of Jews in Berlin. He said they were treated very well. I knew this was a lie because I had had reports from many Russian Jews in Tientsin who had heard from relatives in Berlin. But I took it all down. I also told Dr. Betz that I was becoming homesick for the United States but did not know how I was going to be able to get there because of the cost of Dollar Line steamers. When I discussed my story with Da Costa, I told him I thought Betz's comments about persecution of the Jews were all a pack of lies. Da Costa said, "Well, they are direct quotes from him, so I'm obliged to print them just as he said. We can always blame him if there's anything wrong with them." A few days later I wrote the story as he gave it to me with the lies all carefully reported.

I had a phone call from Dr. Betz. He said he liked the story. He said, "I have an idea. The Germans have a freighter calling at Dairen soon to bring grains and other things along the way back east around through Singapore, the Suez and the Mediterranean to Rotterdam in Holland. Would you have $145? It carries 120 passengers besides its freight. It's the *S.S. Fulda,* a 10,000-ton freighter. I would be glad to get you a passage on the next sailing from Dairen in March. What do you say?" Of course I immediately accepted.

On March 15 Alex Haymon and Carlos Da Costa and Bob Hu, my Chinese assistant on sports coverage, gave me a fine Chinese farewell dinner during which I received all kinds of nice compliments. I was deeply touched by that delightful dinner with my friends I had worked with, and grateful, as I told them, for all the things they had taught me about the newspaper business during that year. It really did sadden me to leave them and I will never forget any of that year. About the same time a reporter on the German paper in Tientsin wrote a farewell editorial about me and that pleased me, too.

So on March 20, 1934, I boarded the little Japanese steamer *Nitto Maru* and made one last trip down the little Hai Ho River to Taku Bar and on across the Bay of Chihli to Dairen where I found my ship the *S.S. Fulda,* that I would be on for the next thirty days. Dr. Betz had got me a single inside cabin. Off we went that night for our first stop in Kobe, Japan.

We stopped overnight in Kobe in its little bay. A New York friend took me to a fine Japanese restaurant in that jewel of a city, Kyoto, where I took my shoes off and left them outside the door. Two stunning geisha girls in their gorgeous beflowered regalia sat with us at a table six inches high.

Next day I took a train to Yokohama to catch up with the *Fulda.* We crossed the China Sea to Shanghai where I watched thousands of coolies carry our cargo past the tallyman who counted each one and handed him his pennies.

Another day the *Fulda* put in at Manila Bay. There I had a drink at the U.S. Army Club's bar which I was told was the longest bar in the world. Then there was the passage from Hong Kong through endless lagoons to Singapore where the heavy odor of spices was everywhere.

I went to the local beach in Singapore which had a fence stretched around it with a sign stating "Watch Out For Sharks Beyond the Fence." A Reuters friend and I dined, of course, at the Raffles Hotel where I sat staring into space and pretending I was Somerset Maugham. At Singapore we picked up many English and Dutch passengers leaving for England and Holland on their long-home-leave. I bought a comfortable rattan pad on which I slept on the open deck of the *Fulda* across the serenest of oceans, the Indian. And so on we went to the Red Sea through the Suez Canal to Suez and on into the Mediterranean.

Finally we reached Casablanca making a shore excursion there. I walked into a section called "bousbier," which was a bordello maintained for the French army soldiers. I was surrounded by some thirty screaming girls seeking business. They followed me toward the exit gate where they were stopped by army police with rawhide whips.

In April we landed in Rotterdam. I left the *Fulda* and my friends and took a train for Paris.

Chapter Eighteen

THE PARIS HERALD

THE DATE WAS April 11, 1934, when the *Fulda* moved slowly up the crowded harbor of Rotterdam on the Lek River near the mouth of the Rhine which flowed into it. I made a visit to Rotterdam's fine zoo and then to the railroad station. Because I was running short of cash I bought a third-class ticket to Paris. The train moved through the pleasant farmlands of Flanders to Brussels.

One of my bachelor friends in Tientsin had advised me to stop in Paris at the Hotel de Sennes on the Rue de Seine which had a nice Restaurant des Arts across the street not far from the Café Flore which my friend said was a gathering place for many of the American newspapermen working in Paris.

During our brief stop in Brussels while the engine was loading coal, I walked to a little park which contained the Mannequin Pis, the most famous scatological work of art in the world. It was a bronze statue of an eight-year-old boy relieving himself proudly in a bowl at his feet. As I looked at the sculpture I thought of another eight-year-old boy relieving himself in Aunt Mary's hall into her umbrella stand.

So my train continued among France's lovely plane trees to the Gare St. Lazare which I remembered well from our visits there on our band trips. I took a taxi from the Gare and asked the driver to take me over the Pont Neuf and on behind the Palais de Justice to Notre Dame on its island on La Cite. I spent half an hour gazing at the overwhelming presentation of French creative imagination as shown by that noble edifice. In writing of the French I should add that I would come to admire them above all other Europeans. But I would never manage really to understand them. They are the French . . . eternally and indivisibly."

I continued onto the left bank and up to my Hotel de Sennes with a glance at the Restaurant des Arts across the street and so on up the Boulevard de St. Germain des Prés past the church and the Café Deux Magots to the Café Flore. I took a table in the sunlight and asked the garçon in my horrible American accent for café-au-lait and croissants. A nice looking man at a table next to me leaned over with a smile and said, "I'll bet you just came in from the States. Welcome aboard, my friend. My name is Elliot Paul. I write novels that nobody reads." We shook hands. Just then a small dark-haired man slunk by moodily and disappeared inside the Flore. Paul said, "Would you believe it? He's got a harem of beautiful girls up in Montmartre, several of which he is married to. Do you know who he is? Pablo Picasso, the world's most famous painter."

I told him, "I just came from China where I was working as a reporter on a newspaper there, and I was hoping that I might find a job on the *Paris Herald*. Elliot Paul told me, "Larry Hills who publishes the *Paris Herald* has been firing most of his reporters in recent months because of the devaluation of the dollar by Roosevelt. The seven-cent franc has made living in Paris so costly that most of the Americans who have been living here had to leave and go home. The tourist business has been practically non-existent." Elliot Paul continued, "But never mind, go ask Larry Hills. You never can tell. You can get there by taking the D bus that stops where those people are. Get yourself a boarding number at that bus post and get off the bus at Rond Pointe. From there walk a block or two up the Champs-Élysées to the Rue du Berri. You will find the *Paris Herald* across the street from the California Hotel. I hope you have good luck." "I hope so, too," I told Paul, "because I am just about out of money."

The people boarded the bus according to the numbers they held in their hands. When I arrived at the new building which housed the *Paris Herald,* a young French boy appeared from what I thought was probably the newsroom and took me into the Lawrence Hills office which faced on the Rue du Berri. He greeted me with a smile and said, "I suppose you may be asking for a job, and I have to tell you that I have nothing for you because we have had to cut our staff drastically lately."

In spite of this discouraging reply, I stepped up and laid my clipping book from the *North China Star* on his desk after I had talked a little about working there. I had opened the book at the article I had written about the sergeant in Tientsin and his affection for his mules. Hills leaned forward and ran his finger down the print and I heard him muttering to himself, "That's not a bad lead." Then suddenly he looked up with a smile, "Maybe I can use you after all. Can you come to work on Monday and report to my managing editor Eric Hawkins? I just happened to remember that some months ago we hired William L. Shirer as a reporter, and he has told us that he is leaving soon to take a job with INS News Service in Berlin where I think he hopes to try broadcasting on Hitler's rise for NBC. You probably need some money, Sprague," Hills said. "Here's your salary for a week, seven-hundred francs." So I left on that day on the Rue du Berri walking on the same kind of air I had walked on so many years ago at Lawrenceville when Jack Sickle released me after a lecture on my bad behavior in stealing his hat.

On Monday morning I rode the D bus around the Place de la Concorde up to Rond Pointe and on to the *Paris Herald* and into the newsroom to Eric Hawkins's big desk at one end of it. I liked Eric Hawkins on sight, a smallish, brisk, neat man who spoke on the phone to somebody in beautiful vernacular French flavored charmingly with a tinge of a British accent. He took me to the copy desk of the long newsroom and introduced me to the copy editor Tommy Thompson. From the copy desk there were two lines of tables with Royal typewriters for the reporters. I met Barbara Fields, the society editor and Artie Young, the movie critic, and a swarthy, corpulent man named Boujea who wrote editorials on French politics.

Meanwhile a tiny little man slipped by us without a word and walked into a small room beyond the copy desk. Erie Hawkins said, "That's Sparrow Robertson, our sports columnist." This Sparrow wore a felt hat that was too big for him, and his suit looked as though he had slept in it. Eric told me, "Sparrow is more famous than the *Paris Herald*. He came to us after the War, and he is a mystery. I think he was born in Brooklyn and did something with boxing or sports there, but he knew every sports personality in the world, or seemed to at the time. That has been his specialty ever since. His column, "Sporting Gossip Column" sounds a little weird in its strange syntax, but it is widely read. At first we had the proofreaders correct it until we found that it was one of the main reasons why people read the *Paris Herald*. So we ordered the proofreaders to keep his "old pal" syntax intact, not to mention his habit of calling everybody's wife "your dear missus."

Eric Hawkins then introduced me to a very slender, rather shy man, a little older than I. "This is Al Laney," Eric said. "He is our tennis reporter and has made quite a name for himself covering tennis in Europe writing of such people as Suzanne Lenglen and Rennie LaCoste, the French star, to say nothing of the women like the marvelous Helen Wills, and Alice Marble, the American stars."

I was dismayed when I bungled the first story that Tommy Thompson assigned me to cover, a race of American motor boats near Paris. It had attracted a large crowd and something happened during the race. My French was so bad that I could not find out what it was. I went back and found that one of the American motorboat racers had fallen off the boat and been killed by a propeller. Tommy Thompson had to get the story from Havas which was the French equivalent of the American AP. He seemed to forgive me. "You'll be able to handle them later."

Meanwhile I had met a dozen other American reporters at the Restaurant des Arts and at the Café Flore. I think I should make very plain that the Paris I came to in April of 1934 was a far cry from the great days of the 1920s that I had read so much about, the wild doings of F. Scott Fitzgerald, Ernest Hemingway and others. The 1920s were lush days when everyone had plenty of money, but in 1934 they did not. Even Joe Zellie's night club was no longer operating and in general we newspaper people were so intent on holding our jobs because of the Depression then in the United States that we didn't kick up our heels very much. We lived rather conservative lives. I don't remember a great deal of drinking. We did gather at the Flore in the evenings and play a little chess or bridge and then went to bed early rather than spending time and money at the Moulin Rouge or Fred Payne's in Montmartre or the Dôme in Montparnasse. But I heard a lot about the old days from a few who had stayed, like Arthur Moss, a tiny little man who had written often about the glory days of the 20s and knew a lot about people like Gertrude Stein and the rest who had participated in those days.

I was particularly helped by a dear ancient lady named Celina Yorke who had written a society column. Whenever I wanted to know about anybody, Celina knew all about the scandals of the dukes, princesses and the rest of them.

During that summer of 1934, I routinely covered the American embassy down by the Hotel Creon where I had a very good friend Robert Murphy who gave me the embassy news. Then I also covered Pershing Hall, the Veterans of Foreign Wars headquarters building near the Rue du Berri. I was also assigned regularly to the monthly meeting of the American Club of Paris which owned a clubhouse on the Champs-Élysées, a few blocks from the Rue du Berri. They usually had a prominent speaker at their luncheons which I was to cover.

My greatest blessing and luck during that first year of my work was knowing my city editor Tommy Thompson, and an excellent headline writer named Hamilton Russell who was among the gifted few who know how to write the heads that make people want to read a piece. I had told Thompson how I had enjoyed writing feature articles without really knowing how. Tommy Thompson decided that he would show me how and since he read all my copy and always gave it the red pencil, he told me what was wrong with my leads and in general just taught me the whole trick of feature writing. He also took care to assign me to interview people and write stories that would give me a chance to practice feature writing.

Meanwhile, the *Paris Herald* did take the *New York Herald Tribune* which came in every couple of weeks. I studied especially the column written by Lucius Beebe, "This New York," which I found most entertaining and decided to try to emulate his style to some degree. Another writer and reporter for the *Herald Tribune* was Joseph Alsop who had created a new style of informal interview. I admired it and tried to use his technique to make people come to life a little when I interviewed them. Tommy Thompson recognized that impulse of mine and tried to encourage me to give it expression. He saw to it that interviews came my way. Because of the idea that Americans had of Paris as the most glamorous city in the world, celebrities coming from the U.S.A. were pleased to be interviewed even by a reporter from the *Paris Herald*.

To learn the history of the *Paris Herald* I went down to Sylvia Beach's famous Shakespeare and Company bookstore in the Boulevard de L'Odéon. She was a charming lady of delightful innocence of expression, manner and dress. I was always amused that she became immortal as the publisher of Joyce's novel *Ulysses* which had been banned from entry into the United States as a pornographic book.

I learned from Al Laney's history that the *Herald* had been started in

October 1887 by James Gordon Bennett, an elegant playboy who was the son of the founder of the *New York Herald Tribune* in the 1850s. In the first issue he published a letter to the editor signed "Old Philadelphia Lady." That letter asked the reader to explain the way to convert the temperature from centigrade to Fahrenheit and vice versa. That query appeared in the *Herald* on December 24, 1899, and elicited immediate response. As a consequence James Gordon Bennett repeated it every day exactly as it was in every issue thereafter for eighteen years. In the process it made the *Paris Herald* famous and continued to do so well into the 1930s. Eric Hawkins said, "We still publish it now and then to this day."

So I came to realize that the fame of the *Paris Herald* depended not alone on its quality but also on that ancient letter of the old Philadelphia lady, plus the daily semi-literate column of Sparrow Robertson on sports figures.

Chapter Nineteen

SKINNY DIPPERS

I HAD SPENT my first few weeks on *The Paris Herald* memorizing the routes of the excellent Paris bus system. I liked to ride in the rear of the bus gripping the hand rail where I could see in all directions the Paris scene as the bus passed through it. I also found the Paris Metro a splendid way to get around, with maps in every station showing the different routes. It was spotless and beautiful in contrast to the disgraceful American subway in New York where people were pressed in like sardines and men hurried to sit in ladies' laps to avoid having to hang from the straps.

Tommy Thompson assigned me to cover the activities of all the Americans in Paris. I remember attending the funerals of former president Raymond Poincaré and of the Minister of Foreign Affairs, Louis Barthou and the annual meetings of the Paris Chamber of Commerce attended by the President of France, Flandin, and, of course, the ambassador Isadore Strauss. The ambassador objected violently to my story about one Chamber of Commerce meeting in which I referred to Flandin's address, pointing out that he spoke with a British accent. That enraged Strauss so that he told Larry Hills that I was banned from entering the embassy. That ban lasted nearly a month when my friend Robert Murphy arranged that I be allowed in again.

I tried writing a story quoting French wine merchants about the utter ignorance of Americans about French wine and how it should be handled. Also I wrote a piece on the business of concierges who always watched at the entrance of apartments to monitor those coming and going. I never did find out the origin of the practice except that it dated from at least the seventeenth century.

I was especially thrilled in the summer of 1934 when Tommy Thompson sent me to cover the launching of France's tremendous, glorious ship the *Normandie.* I also was pleased to be sent to Verdunne where General Pershing addressed a crowd of French veterans and told them that the United States would come to the aid of France once again if they were threatened by Germany or anybody else. That quotation was passed on all over the United States.

I became tired of riding buses and bought from one of the *Herald's* proofreaders a 1925 Citroen three-seated topless roadster for three hundred francs. It was about eighteen horsepower, but it still got me around though I had trouble getting a French license until I realized what was wrong with my replies—I didn't tip the inspector. Then I promptly got my license, which I still have. I drove that little car once to Bruges in Belgium and again to the cathedral on the Loire in Orleans. I became very fond of the little car, although it was hard put to reach a speed of over thirty miles an hour.

I wrote several successful stories about Thomas Jefferson's stay in Paris while he was minister there. His residence happened to be near the Rue du Berri near the *Herald* office. My story attracted so much attention that the authorities posted a plaque on the building that stood on the site that had been Jefferson's home.

I was bored to death by Tommy Thompson's assignment to go all day to the Palais du Justice to attend the trial of Stavisky who had perpetrated the largest financial fraud in French history.

A little later I returned to the Palais du Justice to attend a trial of a night club dancer named Joan Warner, who, as it turned out, was the sister of the Jerry Warner who had been my friend in Tientsin. Joan had been arrested for dancing completely nude at the popular Bal Tabarin night club. The Parisian papers had a great time with that story because the Americans were always making unkind remarks about the immorality of Parisians with their prostitution and the custom of many husbands to have a mistress or two on the side. Joan Warner was tried in the Palais du Justice with all the august justices attending. Her defense was that she wasn't really nude, and they demanded proof of that. The G-string that she claimed concealed her nudity was rather slim, and I was overjoyed to get a picture of one of the dignified justices holding up Joan's covering to the light to see if he could see through it. Apparently they decided that she was after all somewhat covered. They let her off with a five hundred-franc fine.

Another one of my stories described how, after 115 years, the renowned marble statue in the Louvre of the Venus de Milo (or Aphrodite) was moved in an electric car to a better and higher pedestal to the left of the Daru stairway. The Salon de la Venus de Milo had been closed for the time being while Louvre authorities completed the reorganization of the museum's Greek and Roman antiquities.

One of my story assignments which the French papers picked up had to do with the occasion when the governor of South Carolina appointed the president of the American Club of Paris, painter Gilbert White, a colonel, and at the same time bestowed the same honor on Gertrude Stein. White and Stein were highly amused by the appointment but were somewhat surprised when the French government took the appointment seriously and sent secret service men to guard White's apartment and Stein's home on the Rue de Fleurus.

I saw my first preview of television by a pioneer in its development at the American Club. I listened to Louis Bleriot, France's equivalent of Lindbergh and the first man to fly across the English Channel, who predicted that the time was soon coming when passenger planes would be running in eighteen hours from New York to Paris and back again.

As you can imagine I particularly enjoyed covering a concert by the trumpeter Louis Armstrong at the Salle Rameau with a pickup band of various black musicians living in Paris. The hall was jammed and Louis performed beautifully as usual with his white handkerchief waving here and there and his wonderful singing. He also had a marvelous piano player accompanying him, Herman Chittison, who played regularly with the Willie Lewis band at Chez Florence's nightclub in Montmarte.

Whenever stories were slow, especially on Sundays, I could always count on getting something interesting out of the marvelous Gertrude Stein whose book *The Autobiography of Alice B. Toklas* was already a classic. Gertrude was a robust lady in her sixties who loved to talk. She always managed to say something that brought her a lot of American publicity. One of the most famous examples of this was in an avant-garde publication *Transition* where she described the painter Henri Matisse's wife as follows: "Madame Matisse is a very straight, dark woman with a long face and a firm, large, loosely hung mouth like a horse." That certainly did not please Matisse. By way of apology to Henri Matisse Ms. Stein said, "I am very fond of horses and thought my description was a compliment to Madame Matisse." As you can imagine Henri Matisse felt otherwise and I believe he never spoke to Gertrude Stein again if he could help it.

During the summer of 1935 Carl Brandt and his bride Carole Hill honeymooned in Paris and had me escort them to the city's best restaurants. I took them to Maxim's and Fayot's and Prunier's near the Ritz and Escargot near Les Halles and the Rochambeau at Rond Point. We also went to the Flore and the Brasserie Zipp across the street for apertifs.

By day Tommy Thompson kept me busy with feature article assignments. I especially enjoyed covering the luncheons at the American Club of Paris. I enjoyed writing many of my interviews especially the one I wrote about the artist Paul Chabas defending his painting of a nude seventeen-year-old girl which he titled "September Morn." Chabas complained that the Americans were so hypocritical that though they claimed to disapprove of nudity, "September Morn" adorned advertising calendars in every kitchen in America.

I wrote feature stories for Tommy Thompson about crazy things like the American who thought that the frogs' legs served by French restaurants were too small. He went to Louisiana and captured several huge Louisiana frogs with the idea of raising "a billion frogs for French restaurants by 1938." The frogs could not stand the sea voyage and died before he could put his scheme into operation.

Another interview I enjoyed in August of 1934 was with Dorothy Thompson who was married to Sinclair Lewis at the time. She was thrown out of Nazi Germany by Adolf Hitler because some of her newspaper articles were less than enthusiastic about that dictator.

One of my early stories anticipated a new idea that would catch fire among the women of America. It was about Mrs. Floyd Odlum who took over the management of the Bergdorf-Goodman department store in New York at a time when most Americans did not believe that women had enough sense to run anything as complicated as a chicken house let alone the most successful department store in the United States.

I was very glad when Bill and Tesch Shirer asked me if I wanted to take over their apartment of 18 rue Bonaparte. It was in what must have been a fashionable townhouse of some wealthy Parisian and was the place where Mazarek in 1917 had announced the formation of the Czech Republic. It was also rumored that Oscar Wilde had died there.

Della Grace Cochran Sprague, mother of the author.

Joseph Taylor Sprague, the author's father.

Aunt Mary (Mary Aplin Sprague), who wrote a best-selling novel, *An Ernest Trifler,* in 1879.

The author, age three, and his sister, Josephine Taylor Sprague.

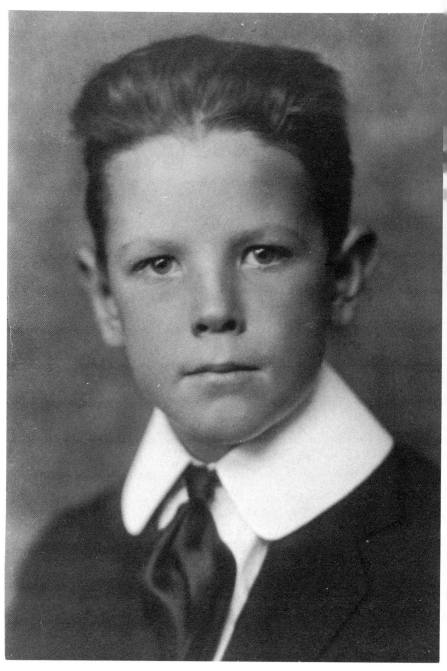

The infamous Buster Brown collar, worn by Marshall Sprague, age eight.

Cowboy Sprague in full regalia from his Valley Ranch adventure.

EJ Sprague, ardent angler, with smallmouth bass she pulled from the South Branch of the Potomac River near Romney, West Virginia where she was born.

M. S. with his trusty Royal typewriter, trying very hard to look like an important writer.

Marshall and EJ Sprague dressed for a
Beaux Arts Ball at the Fine Arts Center

The M. Sprague family—Joe on hood, EJ and Marsh in seat, Steve and Sharon in
rumble—at a Garden of the Gods overlook. The car is Marshall's beloved 1931 Model
A "Calliope."

The apartment was on the fifth floor, up three wide marble stairways to the third floor with, above that, two more floors up a very narrow wooden stairway leading to what I supposed had been the servants' quarters. My little apartment was there, a hundred and two stairs from the bottom. It had a nice little living room with a pot-bellied charcoal stove and a tiny little bedroom with a bed facing the open window overlooking the Beaux-Arts student building. From my wide window I had an unobstructed view of the Eiffel Tower rising in its grandeur perhaps a mile or two in the distance. I had a tiny kitchen with an oil burner and also a tiny bathroom. It was a neat little apartment where I would live for the rest of my two years on the *Paris Herald*. The rent was very reasonable because it had belonged originally to an Englishman who had served in the French Army, and they had given him the privilege of renting it at the reduced rental rates granted to ex-servicemen.

Even though my friends and I were not the boisterous crowd of the 1920s, occasionally we felt like doing something more daring. On Bastille Day when Parisians were celebrating their national holiday on July 14, 1935, my friend Bob, a girl named Maggie (who sent reports on French fashion shows to dress shops in New York) and I piled into the little Citroen and drove around to see how the French were celebrating their holiday. We watched the French girls and boys dancing in the streets outside every cafe. We listened to them roaring out their national anthem. We had brought a bottle of one of my favorites, the Rhone wine Chante Allouette, and went to a picnic table near the base of the Eiffel Tower. After finishing that bottle, we stared at the noble tower rising into the starry sky. It was a warm night and one of us (I don't know which one) thought we ought to do something in honor of that noble tower. We decided to go to the Bois de Boulogne and go swimming in the Racing Club pool. It was the most exclusive social club in Paris. Into the Citroen again we went and into the shadowy Bois to the pool of the Racing Club. As we had hoped, nobody was there. The members were no doubt celebrating the holiday on the Riviera. We climbed the low fence, took off our clothes, hung them on the diving board and dived into the pool, swimming a few lengths with our version of the Australian crawl. We climbed out of the pool feeling a bit more sober than when we went in.

I had never thought of Maggie as especially attractive, but when she lifted her slender, nude body out of the pool and faced us with a gay wave of the hand I realized she was stunningly assembled. She had a neat subtle feminine beauty that the world's great artists have always celebrated in their works as contribution to mankind.

We told each other that it wouldn't be very good for us if the police should find us there and arrest us for trespassing and haul us off to jail, meanwhile, telling Havas that those crazy Americans who were always criticizing the French for immorality were caught skinny-dipping in the Racing Club pool. Havas would send one of the best stories of the year to the Associated Press for dissemination throughout the United States. Fortunately the police did not arrive. We put on our pants and got into the Citroen once more and moved quietly out of the Bois de Boulogne and got back to our rooms safely.

Chapter Twenty

À Bientôt, Paris

O CCASIONALLY ON Wednesday, which was my day off, I went around on a pub crawl in my Citroen by myself to take notes on the behavior of American tourists in Paris in the 1930s. I would stop at Harry's Bar for a glass of milk and then go up the Rue Blanche to Fred Payne's Bar. Fred Payne was an Englishman who specialized in English prostitutes. After Fred Payne's I might wander over to the Café du Dôme on the Boulevard Montparnasse and then to the Little Dango Cafe near the Café Monaco where lesbians had their headquarters.

The most elaborate bordello in Paris was near the Monaco. It was said to be owned by a French senator and was called the Sphinx. I had heard that the senator encouraged American tourists to visit his place to observe that side of Paris high life. I might stop in at the Sphinx and sit at the bar facing the Sphinx's elaborate selection room which re- minded me of the lobby of the Biltmore Hotel in New York. Tea would be served at 5:00 P.M. on tables chastely draped with white linen covers. I would sit watching the American tourists at their tables with their bug-eyed wives watching the "poules" (which is French for prostitute) strolling provocatively past their husbands. I tried to im- agine how the wives would describe their adventure at the Sphinx to their Junior League friends in Keokuk, Iowa. I never stayed very late on these pub hops, and got back to my apartment on the run up the 102 steps before the lights which the concierge had turned on when I came in, went out. Two minutes were all the French apartment owners al- lowed their tenants to save electricity.

Occasionally one of the feature articles Tommy Thompson assigned to me turned out to be a fake story. A shop owner on the Rue de Rivoli phoned him one day that he was about to commit suicide by being squeezed to death by a boa constrictor. I hurried down to the shop and sure enough found the man. His assistant was already in the shop with a large boa constrictor wrapped around his waist. The assistant told me that he had bought the boa from the Samaritaine Department Store near there. They were having a sale of snakes by the yard, he said. Then he handed the importer a bill for the boa for a thousand francs, requiring immediate payment. The importer changed his mind at once about committing suicide. He told his assistant to take the snake back to the Samaritaine on the double.

The feature story that I enjoyed writing for Tommy Thompson had to do with French heroes that were not French at all. Napoleon, my story said, was of Italian origin. The heroic Marshall Ney, who died in 1815, was a Saarlander. General Thomas Arthur Lally was an Irishman as was Marshal Marie-Edme-Patrice-Maurice de MacMahon who was President of the French Republic. Marshall Jaques-Etienne MacDonald was a Scotch-Irish baron. Baron Von Cloots had Dutch-Prussian parents.

After I had debunked various French heroes I wrote a separate debunking piece about the things Napoleon was supposed to have built which he didn't build at all. He was said to have begun the Arc de Triomphe in 1805, but it was finished by King Louis-Philippe in 1836. He was said to have built the Rue de Rivoli in honor of his victory over the Austrians in Rivoli in 1797. It was actually built by Napoleon III in 1865. He didn't build the beautiful Arc du Carousel—he stole it from Venice in 1806. He was said to have built the north end of the Louvre in 1801. That wing was completed in 1823 by King Louis XVIII. Nobody knows who built the Arc de Triomphe but it was a favorite roosting place for some sixteen hundred pigeons. Frenchmen say that these birds behave with great dignity because so many decorous ceremonies take place on top of the arch which has 273 steps to reach the top of it. I counted them.

Tommy Thompson kept me busy writing feature stories, then put me to writing interviews with celebrities. The *Paris Herald* in 1934 was not much of a paper because of reduced advertising. It crammed its news into ten pages or less. Its circulation was probably less than ten thousand, and still the paper maintained its prestige. Celebrities coming from New York to Paris wanted to be mentioned in the paper.

My first interview was with Lily Pons who was staying at the Hotel Choiseul. Miss Pons and her secretary met me in their negligees. The secretary from Cincinatti had gone swimming at Buckeye Lake. After some talk with Miss Pons about her successes in Metropolitan Opera, she left the room and returned in a different negligee, which she said she had just bought at the Gallerie-Lafayette, and asked me how I liked it. Its skirt was slit to the waist and, of course, I said I thought it was grand. After some more uplifting talk about opera I thanked them and left.

Next Tommy sent me to interview John O'Hara whose novel *Butterfield Eight* had just hit the best seller list and had set a new standard in realistic writing. We met at the bar of the Georges Cinque Hotel near the Rue du Berri. O'Hara was wearing a Lacoste suit and seemed to me more like an Ivy League undergraduate than a best-selling novelist. We talked of this and that.

My next interview was one that I would never forget. It was at the Hotel Atlantique near the Arc de Triomphe with the Russian composer and pianist Sergei Rachmaninoff. He received me kindly. He was a tremendously lean and tall man with a long sorrowful face. He asked me where I was from in Ohio, and what life was like in Newark. I could hardly get much out of him during the interview because he kept asking me questions. I told him about Aunt Mary's Tuesday Club and about the bridge clubs and work of the ladies' aid societies who worked as volunteers at Newark's hospitals. He had plied me with questions about Newark for about half an hour. I watched Rachmaninoff's long fingers and could imagine why he could use them at the keyboard with such wonderful dexterity. As I walked away, Rachmaninoff said, "Your Newark sounds a lot like the village where I was born, Novgorod." I experienced a burst of exultation as I recalled that this great man from Russia had chosen to become an American citizen.

I will mention only briefly the many interviews that Tommy Thompson assigned to me during the rest of my two years as a *Paris Herald* reporter. I particularly enjoyed an interview with Strangler Lewis, the famous American wrestler. After he had explained to a group of French students how to become a wrestling champion, he told me later that wrestling had turned out during his career to be a lot like politics. "It has its ups and downs," he said, "just like President Roosevelt. You win some, you lose some." In the same vein when Babe Ruth came to town I covered his talk to a class of French school children who asked him how he managed to hit so many home runs. Babe Ruth told them, "You just stand there at the plate and when the pitcher throws the ball at you, you close your eyes and swing hard and hope you hit something."

I interviewed the famous English socialist Bertrand Russell in a cafe near the Sorbonne Observatory. Russell told me that industrial magnates in the steel industry were to be blamed for manipulating the nations into war. "Adolf Hitler," he said, "is just a megaphone for the German iron and steel business. I admit he does well with his megaphone, but that is because the Germans still believe he is also very competent."

I interviewed the explorer Lincoln Ellsworth who was about to attempt his last great adventure, an attempt to fly over Antarctica. I interviewed Rafael Sabatini whose fiery novel *Scaramouche* has scared the wits out of me with its violent action. Sabatini had just been married. He turned out to be the gentlest, mildest, most modest man I had ever met, in startling contrast to his novels.

I interviewed the great American war aviator, Edward Vernon Rickenbacker. He told me, "Nobody would believe me, but I can tell you that a few years from now the Pacific Ocean will be crisscrossed by passenger airplanes flying by way of Hawaii at a speed that would make Lindbergh's epochal crossing of the Atlantic in 1927 seem like no feat at all."

I especially enjoyed interviewing Borah Minovitz, a thirty-two-year-old man in Kiev, Russia, who had become in the United States the king of harmonica players. He delighted me with his skill on his twelve-tone harmonica playing almost anything including "Rhapsody in Blue." Minovitz gave me one of his twelve-tone harmonicas which he had invented so he could play classical or jazz music.

I did not manage to arrange an interview with the Duke of York, who later became the King of England, but I did attend a large dinner in his honor at the Gare D'Orsay, seated far away from him at the press table. During his talk the Duke, who was born with a stutter, suddenly stopped talking and for two endless minutes just stood there while his audience endured with him the pain of his embarrassment. Finally he conquered his stutter and continued his speech. That Duke of York had plenty of courage, we decided.

Of the several Hollywood movie stars I interviewed like Grace Moore or Laura La Plante, none thrilled me as much as the thirty-year-old Austrian beauty, Elissa Landi. I was so stunned by her looks that I could not read the notes I had made about her.

I was not pleased to meet William Lyon Phelps, the Yale University professor. I met him in the Hotel Continental lobby. As I walked towards him he said to me, "Sprague, I know you went to Princeton from the way you walk." I asked him, "How was that?" He said, "Well, it's a sort of a casual stroll as though you thought that any girl watching you would swoon at the sight of you."

As I moved into the late fall of 1935, I began to worry about my health. I was losing weight. I had days of fatigue when it was hard for me to do my interviews. I began to be homesick for the United States.

At this time Tommy Thompson instructed me to interview Kathleen Norris who was the country's most successful writer of magazine serials. Her husband Charles G. Norris wrote novels, too. I wrote a silly lead for my interview with Mrs. Norris which read: "The two phenomena of the twentieth century, Soviet Russia and Kathleen Norris, met last week and after an exchange of impressions concluded that both were what they were cracked up to be. Of the two, Soviet Russia should have been awed the most because whereas 168 million people had created Soviet Russia, Mrs. Norris had created herself all by herself." Kathleen and Charles G. Norris had arrived in Paris with a Persian kitten named Piper who spent most of its time chewing the pencils which Kathleen used to outline her serials which she wrote every three months for the *Ladies' Home Journal* and *Collier's*.

Charles G. Norris must have liked my interview because he asked me to have dinner with him. I took him to my favorite night club, Chez Florence's in Montmartre because I liked Willie Lewis's Dixieland band that played there. As Norris and I were having dinner at a table near the door, he nudged me when two people walked into the club. Norris said, "Do you know who that is? That's Marilyn Miller, New York's musical comedy star. The handsome man with her is George Charpentier, the French boxer. I saw him get knocked out in the fourth round at Madison Square Garden by Jack Dempsey in 1920." Charpentier was a handsome, powerfully built man, and of course, Marilyn Miller was beautiful.

With their appearance out of the way, I told C. G. about my wishes to become a writer. He told me that I ought to leave my reporter job at the *Paris Herald* and move to New York where all the publishers and literary agents were, like Carl Brandt and go on from there. Then he made a surprising suggestion. "If you will leave and come to San Francisco on July 15, 1936, I will take you with me as my guest to an annual summer camp of writers that I belong to. I think that would be good for you as you will find several authors there who will advise you about the writing business. They call it the Bohemian Club."

And so early in January I regretfully told Lawrence Hills and Eric Hawkins that I would have to leave Paris and go home. They came to have a farewell drink with me in my apartment. After they had gone I discovered that Larry Hills, who had tried out the twelve-tone harmonica that Borah Minowitch gave me, had put it in his pocket and absconded with it.

I arranged passage to New York on the *U.S.S. Manhattan* in a large stateroom. It didn't cost very much because I had always been very careful to mention the steamship line in my copy when their ships arrived from New York.

Chapter Twenty-One

CALIFORNIA, HERE I COME

I HAD A SMOOTH, late January 1936 crossing on the *U.S.S. Manhattan*. I noticed at the captain's table William Philipps, the ambassador to Italy, and the famous foreign correspondent in Moscow for the *New York Times,* Walter Duranty, and also Frazier Hunt from the wire services.

I had a pang of nostalgia as the *Manhattan* moved into New York harbor past the magnificent Statue of Liberty which the French government had given to the United States in 1884. It had been designed in Paris by Bertholdi, and the copper plates of the design were placed on a framework of steel made by Gustave Eiffel, then shipped to the United States as a symbol of Franco-American friendship. The *Manhattan* moved slowly by the 151-foot high statue with its fog horn blowing as a warning to the Staten Island ferry on its way to Manhattan.

I had read somewhere about the statue later, that the key to its door was sent by the government to George Washington's home at Mount Vernon where it is still on display. And so I arrived at the *Manhattan's* dock and carried a box of Rhone wine Meursault that I had bought in Paris as a present for Carl Brandt and my literary mentor Hugh Kahler. I got a taxi at the dock and was impressed immediately as we drove over to Park Avenue by the bigness of everything in the United States, its buildings, its taxis. Unnecessary bigness, I thought, compared to the modest dimensions that I was accustomed to during my two years of residence in Paris. My taxi went up Park Avenue through the two tunnels underneath the enormous Grand Central Station and on into Central Park that ran for miles from 59th Street north to 110th Street at the edge of Harlem and on to my garage at 135th Street and Riverside Drive where I found my Model-A Calliope and charged her battery and found her running as well as ever after being in dead storage for four years while I was abroad.

I drove her on down to 126 West 104th Street and was greeted by Josie and her five-year-old son Erik, and Mother. Josie told me that she and Howie were divorced and I spent some of February playing father to little Erik, taking him to Ringling Brothers three-ring circus in the huge Madison Square Garden and buying him a Lionel electric train.

Josie, meanwhile, and Erik left the apartment and moved to Mexico to the quaint little town of Tasco where a friend of Josie's loaned them the use of an adobe house. I was running short of money, having no job, and neither the *New York Times* nor the *New York Herald Tribune* had any use for a reporter without long experience in the New York scene, but I thought of my feature stories on the Herald, so I went back to the *New York Times* on 43rd Street working my way through a mob of hysterical teenagers lining the sidewalk as they tried to attend a Benny Goodman concert in the Paramount Theater. I went to the sixth floor of the *New York Times* Sunday department and was sent in to the travel editor, George Copeland. He looked over my clipping book and said, "Do you know anything about tropical fish? People are buying a lot of them to install in their penthouse apartments." Of course I said I had an intimate acquaintance with tropical fish, and so I went down into the Bowery and talked to an importer of tropical fish and wrote a story based on his views of the business of importing the colorful fish. George published the story on a Sunday later and paid me $100 for it.

Through that spring I wrote many stories for the Sunday department on a variety of subjects including a magazine story for the *New York Times Magazine* on the Central Park Zoo which was assigned to me by editor of the Sunday department, Lester Markel. He was a perfectionist who monitored every word that went into his Sunday sections and was a severe critic and was not even reluctant to criticize the owners of the *Times* if he thought they weren't running the paper properly. Sometimes when he read his Sunday editions that he had okayed and sent to press, if he found a wrong word or a misspelled word or type, he would have a temper tantrum so violent that he frightened everybody on the sixth floor.

I had the wonderful help of a copy reader named Walter Hayward who read all my copy, blue penciled it and then explained to me why he made the corrections that he did on my copy. He taught me more about writing than anybody else, even Tommy Thompson on *The Paris Herald*. He told me again and again in writing stories to keep them brief and plausible and make sure at the opening that the reader was told what the point of the story was, and also to use very few adjectives and avoid slang and cliches. "Read carefully the style of great writers like Somerset Maugham and John Galsworthy and Walter Scott," he said. Hayward was an Englishman born in Bermuda. I owe him an enormous debt as I do to Hugh Kahler and Carl Brandt for all the time they spent trying to teach me how to write.

In the middle of June 1936, George Copeland noted that the Mexican government was building a modern paved highway that would run from Laredo, Texas, to Mexico City, 720 miles, and would open officially on July 1, 1936. George asked me if I could drive down there and cover that opening of the highway. I had not forgotten that I had promised C. G. Norris before I left Paris that I would meet him at his home in Saratoga, California, and he would take me to the summer encampment of the Bohemian Club in its redwood grove north of San Francisco. Also I could stop and see Josie on my trip to Mexico. So I tuned up the Calliope and set out to cover the Mexican highway and get on to California to meet Charlie Norris.

I always loved traveling in Calliope with the top down and enjoying the beauty of our United States. From New York I traveled to Newark to say hello to Everett D. Reese who asked me, "Do you happen to know how far it is from Newark to Tasco?" "Oh, I don't know," I said. "I suppose it must be around five hundred miles. He said, "You're going to be surprised. It's over two thousand miles." So on I went from Newark down into Kentucky, on to Memphis, Tennessee, across the Mississippi on the bridge at Greenville and so into Louisiana. I remembered that my love that I had lost by her marriage in June of 1932 lived in Alexandria, Louisiana. So I drove through the town out of curiosity and on the outskirts I phoned her home on a pay telephone and was told by whomever answered that she was visiting relatives in the north.

I was trying to make the trip on $90 a month which was all I could spare of money from Dad's estate which I shared with Mother. I would put aside a few dollars a day for meals and whatever I had to spare I spent on gasoline as far as a tankful a day would take me. The going price was twenty cents a gallon. I also carried a package of dog biscuits so that when I stopped at some farmer's yard and got permission to spend the night sleeping beside Cloppy on a cot with a piece of canvas above me in case of rain I could hand out the biscuits if the dog didn't like me. Sometimes the dog even slept with me.

I did not stay long with Josie in Tasco, but I did write the story of the road from Laredo to Mexico City. I had picked up a Mexican boy my age at Laredo to share the driving, and also to do the talking for me in the Mexican language since the road was absolutely empty of all the usual facilities, no gas stations, garages, motels or anything yet. The shovels and building equipment were still operating in the beautiful mountain section that I found just short of Mexico City. My driver and I made it comfortably. We would stop at somebody's house and ask to buy from them as much gasoline as they could spare to carry us along.

In July I knew it was time to head for California by way of Amarillo and the so-called honeymoon route, U.S. 66 through Albuquerque and Flagstaff and Needles. I stopped very briefly at Grand Canyon, that somehow frightening gash where I got material for a story to write for the *Times* travel section. Then I continued over the Mohave Desert in blistering heat through Barstow to Los Angeles and on up to Carpenteria where I spent a day in a motel on the Pacific side and bought new tires and tubes for Calliope at $8 apiece which gives you an idea that the Depression was still on. So to Charlie Norris's large home at Saratoga where I shared a guest house with Charlie's two sons, one of them a doctor and the other a reporter on the *San Francisco Chronicle*. I enjoyed my swims in Charlie's pool, watching Kathleen Norris swimming while she dictated her serials to her secretary seated beside the pool. The *Ladies Home Journal* and *Collier's* bought them at something like $2 a word, so Charlie told me.

So on July 15, Cloppy and I followed Charlie's Cadillac through San Francisco and on some eighty-five miles to the large acreage of redwoods that the Bohemian Club owned on the Russian River.

Signs at the Club's entrance gate stated that autobikes and bicycles were not permitted on the grounds of the grove.

Charlie and I gave our names to the stern guard in his station at the gate. A bus stood there and carried us to Charlie's cabin and tent. I could see the many cabins of members below the towering redwoods beyond it.

Awaiting me in Charlie's cabin was his first guest. It was Richard Halliburton. I had interviewed him twice in Paris where he was still pursuing his "royal road to romance," this time tracking the trail of Hannibal and his elephants from the Alps on his way to conquer Rome in 183 B.C. Another of Charlie's guests arriving that day was Templeton Crocker of an old San Francisco family. Crocker told me when I asked about the Bohemian Club that it was started in 1872 and was the oldest men's club west of the Mississippi. He added that people in San Francisco spoke of its members as "the power elite." Crocker added proudly that its members were wealthy people with cultural interests.

Charlie's guests included the editor of *Fortune Magazine,* Eric Hodgins, who told me his book *Mr. Blandings Builds His Dream House* would be published soon.

I shared a Norris tent with a director of NBC and with John Charles Thomas, a Metropolitan Opera baritone who sang to us often after supper.

I had breakfast the next day outdoors at a long table with wooden benches to sit on. I was enjoying my bacon and eggs. I asked the man sitting beside me to pass the salt, which he did. I turned to thank him. It was Herbert Hoover.

I spent my encampment days at lectures, organ and concert recitals. I swam daily in the Russian River. Sunning themselves near the river a few girls in bathing suits gazed at us intently to see how the members of "the power elite" behaved themselves.

The encampment's big event was the presentation of "High Jinks" which was a serious stage show. Charlie was the author of the 1936 show "Ivanhoe" which was based on Walter Scott's book. The large cast wore tunics and skull caps, dress of the Ivanhoe period. The play was accompanied by musicians from the San Francisco Symphony.

The "Low Jinks" was a series of comedy skits. I spotted Walt Disney watching the skits. He was a smallish, handsome man. I had heard that he had just completed the film "Snow White and the Seven Dwarfs." Disney, I thought, had the benign, gentle kind of face I would expect of the creator of a film like "Snow White."

Before my encampment ended I was delighted to have long talks about writing with Stewart Edward White, a *Post* short-story writer, and Charles Caldwell Dobie who wrote fine stories about the San Francisco Chinese.

I did not meet Irvin S. Cobb, the Paducah humorist and Dad's favorite, who was in poor health. He was there, but did not get around much.

Before I left the grove, I tried to thank Charlie properly for the unforgettable fortnight he had given me. I would see both Charlie and Kathleen Norris often in years to come when they visited their New York suite in the Chatham Hotel.

Chapter Twenty-Two

LOVE IN BLOOM

I WAS EXTREMELY grateful to C. G. Norris for offering me the fortnight at the Bohemian Club, which is a memorable event for me. I tried to tell C. G. how much I appreciated his kindness in inviting me to attend. When I said goodbye to him, I drove the Model-A to San Francisco. I left San Francisco early in August of 1936 on just about the hottest day I ever remember. It was so hot that it exploded the thermometer on the dashboard of the Model-A. It must have been at least 110. When I got to beautiful Yosemite National Park, where I was able to cool off, they had tents for visitors for fifty cents a night. So I got space in a tent there. I was still short of money as I started out on the four thousand miles to New York. I needed to get along on $6.00 a day, spending $3.00 for fifteen gallons of gasoline. The Model-A would carry me about three hundred miles on fifteen gallons.

It was a beautiful drive from Yosemite across the Cascade Range and down to Mono Lake and then across Nevada to Salt Lake City. From Salt Lake I continued into western Wyoming and through Evanston into Rock Springs and across the red Desert to Laramie and to Cheyenne. I had decided to go to Cheyenne, though it would have been shorter to go to Denver. I remembered my third grade teacher Miss Beecher telling us that Denver was a mile-high city and I pictured that as high up in the air with deep canyons and frightening shelf roads that the Model-A might fall off of. I decided to avoid such a dangerous place and go to Cheyenne where there were no mountains.

From Cheyenne I moved on down the North Platte River to Grand

Island in very pleasant weather. I found places to stay at $2.50 a night with all the facilities, including a shower outside. Then to Des Moines, Iowa, and Illinois into Chicago. I had a happy reunion in Chicago with Jack Howe and his lovely wife Mary Lou. I continued from Chicago to New York by going to Erie and Scranton. So the day came when I found myself back in mother's studio apartment on West 104th Street where Josie and her son Erik were also living. As it turned out that would conclude for quite a while my work in foreign lands.

I rested a bit. Then one day the telephone rang and I answered it. A man's voice said, "This is Iron Stomach and Water Lily is with me." It was Steve Ailes and his brother Trouble of the old Nicatous Camp days. They said that they were meeting Sallie Ailes who had been visiting friends in England after Soldier Ailes had died. Edna Jane was with them. So, of course, I jumped into the Model-A and hurried down to 85th Street across Central Park to 5th Avenue and down 5th Avenue and arrived at the 42nd Street bus station of the B & O Railroad. There was my Edna Jane, still as beautiful as I remembered her but very thin. We had lunch at the Princeton Club and I took her down to the Cunard Dock to meet Sallie coming in on the boat. I won't try to tell you how incredibly thrilled I was to see my old girl again and learn from her that she had an amicable breaking up and a divorce was in process in Louisiana which would become final in a few months. She came down soon after our meeting, and we had dinner. We were standing beside the Frigidaire in Mother's kitchen when I asked her to marry me. She said "Yes." So we planned to marry as soon as her divorce was final.

During the waiting period for EJ's divorce to become final, I worked hard for George Copeland at the *Times*. He was very helpful to assign me to write some of my travel stories about places near Martinsburg, West Virginia, where EJ was living with her mother. Soldier had died at Scarborough. The family had sold the big Scarborough house and had moved to Martinsburg, where Steve was practicing law. I wrote stories about the Great Smoky Mountains National Park in Tennessee and the tobacco auctions in North Carolina. Then an extensive story about Rockefeller's colonial Williamsburg which they had just set up.

By coincidence, EJ and I were married on St. Valentine's Day, February 14, 1939. Steve Ailes got everything together, including a United Brethren minister—the Episcopalians would not marry EJ because of her divorce. Steve made reservations on the B. & O. to get us to New

York where we would embark for France the next day. When the train came in, several relatives came to the end of the club car to wave goodbye. In the club car a stranger came up to us, brought us champagne and said, "I understand that your brother-in-law could only get you an upper berth on the Pullman at the last minute. You know you can't spend your wedding night in an upper berth. Here, take my drawing room. I'll take your berth." So we had the luxury of a drawing room for our wedding night.

The next morning in New York I found Ev Reese, trustee of Father's estate, who had come on from Newark to check up on me because I had reservations for our honeymoon in Europe and had borrowed the money from the estate. Then Ev Reese and Josie saw us off on the *President Roosevelt* across the Atlantic. We did not have a visa for France, but George Copeland called the French Tourist Bureau in New York who cabled the customs office in Paris to let us into France without a visa. We had a rather rough crossing, but not any of the fifty-foot waves that I had had in smaller boats in earlier crossings.

On the boat I played chess with the Irish playwright Liam O'Flaherty who got so mad when I beat him that he threw the board into the sea. We made friends with a French official who was in New York buying fighter planes in anticipation of war with a rearmed Germany. He said, "The war is bound to happen soon."

Arriving in Le Havre we went to Paris and on to the Hotel Georges Cinque where we were given a huge room with a bath that had two of everything, as befitted a travel writer for the Sunday edition of *The New York Times*.

That evening I took EJ to the nearby *Paris Herald* to show her to Eric Hawkins and my reporter friends. After they put the paper to bed at 1 A.M., all of us went to a small cafe nearby where Hawkins bought two bottles of champagne in honor of our marriage.

I drank too much champagne. Erik Hawkins had to almost carry me with EJ holding up my other sagging side down the Rue du Berri and across the Champs-Élysées to the Georges Cinque. Next morning, eager to try my horrible French I phoned the hotel's hairdresser for EJ. "Voulez vous arranger ma femme?" I asked. With a giggle he replied, "Mais oui, Monsieur! Je viens immediatement, toute de suite!"

We bought a Citroen roadster at a bargain price—$300.00—from a Frenchman who, like many others, was selling his car because of the threat of German invasion. We had a lovely drive down to the Riviera by way of Vichy and a charming Rhone village where, at the inn, we were served the nation's prize wine, Chante Alovétte.

From there we set out for Monte Carlo, Pisa, Amalfi, Naples, Venice, then to Vienna where we stopped at the Hotel Bristol. But Vienna was terribly depressing since Hitler had taken over Austria and continued his persecution of the Jews. Jewish shops were marked—parks had signs "Juden verboten!" We couldn't stand it, so we decided to get out of there. We got on the autobahn and rushed out of Vienna to Munich and on to Cologne. On Hitler's birthday we got out of Germany, happy to leave having passed endless army camps where Hitler was rearming in violation of the Versailles Treaty.

So we left Cologne happily, going to Bruges in Belgium and then, the next day took the Citroen across the channel to England and began a tour through Wales. Of course, we had been warned at the very start in Paris by an American friend, "Don't you take that trip. That French car will break down somewhere along the way." He had a Packard. Sure enough, it did break down at Holmes Chapel beyond Chester. The left front wheel just fell off at a railroad station. So we took rooms in the station hotel while the wheel was being fixed. Whenever a train would come in the hotel would tremble, tremble, tremble, almost knocking us out of bed. We spent a week or so trembling above the station at Holmes Chapel.

When we got the little Citroen back safely out of England, we spent a few days at the Hotel Lennox in Paris about a block from the Café Flore. Around the first of June 1939, we sadly said goodbye to France and rode the *President Harding* back to New York. From there we drove to Maine to attend Steve's wedding near Belfast where the family of his wife Nellie Wales had a summer place.

Meanwhile EJ and I had rented a house in Martinsburg, West Virginia, where Sallie was. Our first son, Joseph Taylor Sprague, was born there on the 9th of December 1939. Typically I hurried to the wrong hospital to greet Joe.

I had been feeling very weary at the time with all this traveling and found it hard to get out and do my travel stories for the *New York Times*. My fatigue got steadily worse. I began to think strongly that I must have tuberculosis, remembering that Hamilton Russell had coughed a lot while I worked with him on the *Paris Herald*, and that he had died of tuberculosis. I consulted several doctors in Washington and Maryland all that winter of 1940. They did not seem to think I had TB. Finally I consulted Doctor Oswald Jones in New York who said I certainly did have it. He tried to get me assigned to the Trudeau Sanitorium at Saranac, New York, but they said they had no room for me. He said, "I would like to get you to bed right away because you are running a fever. How would you like to go to Colorado Springs? I often send patients to Dr. Gerald Webb out there."

EJ and I talked it over. I had written some stories for the travel section about Colorado. I had written a glowing story about Colorado Springs and the Broadmoor Hotel, and so we said that it wouldn't be a bad idea to see the place I had written about so enthusiastically. It would also be good to get away from the family so they wouldn't be so worried about us while I was being cured from TB.

Chapter Twenty-Three

PIKES PEAK OR BUST

I T WAS A miserable, rainy evening in late March when EJ and Josie took me in a taxi to Grand Central Station and put me on the Lakeshore Limited of the New York Central in a Pullman bound for Chicago and eventually for Colorado Springs. It was a rather bad moment as I stood in the vestibule of the Pullman car marked "Broadmoor" and waved goodbye to EJ and Josie as the Lakeshore Limited began moving slowly out of the station. There were no tears, because I believed that all three of us were relieved that something was to be done at last about the fatigue, weight loss, and listlessness that had bothered me for so many months.

I stayed awake as the train moved into Westchester County and past the Scarborough Station where I could see from the window what had been the Ailes house. I could see the lights of the home where EJ and I had had furious Ping-Pong battles which, of course, the athletic Edna Jane always won. I could imagine the mulberry tree by the house that I had climbed with Soldier standing below watching me and muttering, "Does anybody smell skunk around here?"

Moving through Poughkeepsie I remembered the Vassar junior prom in 1930 that EJ had asked me to attend. I remembered how sick with worry I was all that week because I had driven up to Vassar from Scarborough in EJ's father's beautiful new LaSalle car during a snowstorm. I was afraid that I would wreck the car driving back. Also I worried that EJ's classmates would wonder why she ever invited that uncouth runt who couldn't dance anything but the Princeton one-step instead of some handsome, suave football player from Yale or Harvard.

I had breakfast in the morning as we coasted beyond Buffalo along Lake Erie and on to the LaSalle Street Station in Chicago where I was very pleased to find Jack Howe and his beautiful wife Mary Lou to whom EJ had wired the time of my arrival. Mary Lou was a registered nurse, and there on the platform she took my temperature, pulse and blood pressure, which she said were OK for the two-day trip from Chicago to Colorado Springs on the Rock Island Rocket. They put me on the train.

During the first day of my trip I reviewed what Dr. Oswald Jones had told me about tuberculosis. He said that it had been called consumption through most of the nineteenth century and was a major cause of death in the United States and the rest of the world for that matter. The cause of this infection of the lungs was not known, but in 1882 the German bacteriologist Robert Koch discovered the tubercule bacillus that lodged usually in the lungs where it caused an infection that could spread to other parts of the body. Total bed rest for a year or so allowed the lung to be much less active, and the patient's natural resistance often allowed the tuberculosis infection to slowly heal.

The next day after we passed Omaha, Nebraska, the train moved into the flat, treeless area that early explorers had called "The great American Desert." We pulled later into the Colorado Springs station, and I could see out the train window the reassuring sun-covered shape of 14,000-foot Pikes Peak appearing to be not very far away. My first impression at the station as I looked out was a startling clarity and piney fragrance of the air at six thousand feet above sea level. Everything I looked at was so clear that it almost hurt my eyes, accustomed to the dimmer atmosphere back east.

As I stepped from the train, a magnificent, tall, handsome man who was, of course, Dr. Gerald Webb, told me he had a room for me. "At the Broadmoor Hotel?" I asked. "The Broadmoor," he exclaimed. "Whoever told you that you were going to the Broadmoor? You are going to the hospital here, Glockner Hospital."

As we moved northward up Cascade Avenue in Dr. Webb's Chevy, I noted huge houses on both sides of the street. Dr. Webb said, "Those houses are boarding houses for convalescent TB patients. Notice those window rooms which have been added to the second floor for these patients? The usual treatment here is to put the patient on total bed rest for a year or two so that his natural resistance can begin healing the TB while he is keeping his lungs at rest. And our clear air is very good for him. So they built sleeping porches. The bed rest idea was developed first in Davos, Switzerland, and brought over here from Saranac to Colorado Springs. Of course, patients are required to follow a strict regimen so as not to pass on their germs to healthy people. The tubercule bacillus is very contagious."

Dr. Webb stressed that the Colorado Springs climate did not necessarily cure a person's tuberculosis, but it seemed to help the curing process if the person was in a cheerful environment that would alleviate the boredom of staying immobile in bed for such a long time. Obviously if morale stayed in good shape, resistance to infection would do a better job and help restore health in time.

So we continued up the wide Cascade Avenue and through the spacious campus of Colorado College, which Dr. Webb told me, was started in 1874 by the Civil War General, William Jackson Palmer. General Palmer had also founded the city in 1871 as a summer resort, then later as a health resort. A few blocks beyond Colorado College we came upon the old-fashioned building of Glockner Hospital set in a park lined with several large cottonwood trees.

Dr. Webb said, "Glockner Hospital was built in 1888. Even in the late 1880s doctors had realized that TB patients seemed to do well in Colorado Springs because of the good air and the sunlight."

Dr. Webb took me into the hospital which smelled pleasantly of pine and polish and installed me in a small alcove with a bed in Room 140 with windows on both sides. By that time I was very tired and glad when a nurse came and took my temperature. She put me to bed and asked me what I would like for lunch. Then I fell asleep.

Chapter Twenty-Four

CHASING THE CURE

L ATER ON that afternoon of my first day, a tall, lean black-haired man came in and said he was my orderly, and that his name was Frank Smentowski. He gave me a bed bath and asked me how I was. I said, "Fine." He said, "You don't look fine to me." "Oh, but I am," said I. "I'll be out of here in a couple of weeks." He said, "That's what they all say. Most of them are still around after a couple of years. But don't worry. It just takes time." Frank added, "I came here in 1926 with tuberculosis and stayed in bed a few months until I couldn't afford to pay the hospital for my keep any longer, and they said, 'Well, if you get up and go to work, we'll keep an eye on you.' So I did get up, and I went to work, and I've been here ever since."

When Frank turned to leave I started to get out of bed. He turned around and said, "Don't you dare. You get back in that bed. If you want to go to the bathroom, here's a duck." He handed me the urinal which everybody in those days called a duck because it looked like one. So I immediately got back in bed and that was the last time for a good while that I tried to get up for any reason at all. I must say I felt much better after I had spent a couple of weeks in my alcove and had become used to the hospital routine.

I was happy when EJ finally arrived from Martinsburg, West Virginia, in our Ford station wagon with our son Joe and Vera, our seventeen-year-old nursemaid whom we had brought from her home in Belfast, Maine. EJ managed to find a house to rent at 19 West Boulder Street downtown on a bluff overlooking Memorial Park and Monument Creek and with a full view of Pikes Peak. The house was called

Hobgoblin Hall, an interesting place owned by a man who must have had a psychosis about burglars as every door that was opened or even touched by anybody caused a light to flash over EJ's bed in the large bedroom near my sleeping porch.

Before I left my alcove room at Glockner I gained a half a pound in weight every week and felt much improved about my prospects for getting well. In August after I had been on bed rest for five or six months, Dr. Webb came in and greeted me with "Congratulations, Marshall. You have turned the corner. I think you should join Edna Jane at Hobgoblin Hall." So that's what I did. It was really a joy to be with my family again.

The house had been owned by Chester Alan Arthur, the son of the President of the United States who had come from Paris years ago because of the popularity of polo in Colorado Springs. Colorado Springs had become, at that time, sort of a polo capitol of the West. EJ and I spent our first Colorado New Year's Eve drinking a split of champagne and toasting Pikes Peak through the picture window of the upstairs bathroom at Hobgoblin Hall—the best view in the house. We thought it was the nicest New Year's Eve we'd ever spent.

Meanwhile Colorado Springs received an enormous economic lift when the Army decided to build Fort Carson near the town. The building began on January 1, 1942 and, of course, our landlady raised the rent. EJ found another house on a quiet residential street called Wood Avenue and rented that with an option to buy later if we should decide on that step. In 1941 our second son Steve was born. EJ took our two infant sons back to West Virginia to show them to her mother in Martinsburg. I returned to Penrose in a room on the third floor during her absence.

One day I was overjoyed to receive a letter from my mentor and advisor Hugh MacNair Kahler who had learned of my illness from Carl Brandt. He was writing just after Pearl Harbor. By that time it seemed certain that World War II would not be over soon. His letter said, "Before this mess is over, twice as many people as ever before in world history will have to live in bed to recover from their wounds as you are. The best that you can do is to try to explain what bed rest is all about while you are still in a place to see what it is like." So Frank Smentowski brought me a notebook and pencils, and I began to make notes of my impressions of everything that had happened to me in Glockner up to then.

Then I began to write an article. I titled the piece, "The Great Business of Getting Well." After a month struggling writing it, I sent it along to Carl Brandt in New York. Two weeks later a telegram came from Carl saying "Herbert Mays, the editor of *Good Housekeeping* likes your 'Get Well' article very much and paid me $250 for it. He also told me to have you send him a second article on the same subject." What wonderful news that was and how good for my morale! I had never sold an article to such a first-class magazine in my life.

While I was writing the second article for *Good Housekeeping,* Carl wrote that he had also heard from Bob Crowell asking me to expand the material contained in the magazine articles to a length suitable for a book that he wanted to publish with the title *The Business of Getting Well.* So there it was. I spent the rest of that year on that expansion. My first hardback book was published a year later, and I was delighted to receive some very good reviews of it in *The New York Times Book Review* and many other periodicals.

I should have added that when the first *Good Housekeeping* article was published it was accompanied by a photograph of a man sitting in bed—it was made from a model, of course. But the model was such a handsome man that before that month was over I received fifty letters from readers who fell in love with him and sent me letters practically proposing marriage.

During that time the *Readers' Digest* was publishing several dedications they had found in recently published books. They included my dedication from my little book, which read "For Edna Jane . . . worth a billion hot water bottles . . ."

I will now try to explain how I passed my time in 1941 and 1942 and even later chasing the cure at Glockner Hospital without driving myself crazy because of the inactivity. I remember that when I first had been in that bed for a whole week, I began to comb my memory for popular songs beginning with the first that I could remember which must have been written in 1910, "Has anybody seen my rover?" and I sang that. I also sang, over and over, "Goodbye, Girls, I'm Through." I reconstructed scenes and evenings of my early life as a boy traveler, hero, and even lover. Delightful smells came to mind such as the basement of Dad's grocery where the vinegar and cheeses were stored. I saw Aunt Mary's dressmaking model, name of Matilda, and my grandmother's cream separator. I recalled the time I got jailed at the age of five for housebreaking at home. I thought of that day, a year later, when my dear gentle grandpa asked me to go gather the eggs and I replied with a lovely phrase picked up from the hired man, "Oh, go sit on a tack, you ole son of a bitch."

I also passed a lot of time at Glockner observing the conduct of other patients down the hall. One of them was Joe Potts, a cattleman from Kansas City. Joe was an example of how rugged individualists meet the test of illness. His method was to bone up on his doctor's orders and do the opposite. When Joe was told to hire a nurse and come to Colorado by slow train, he bought a quart of rye and drove himself to Colorado at night, at ninety miles an hour. On his arrival, absolute rest was prescribed, so Joe had a cocktail party for twelve people the next day. Later, he was advised to take fresh air and sun and mild exercise. He closed his windows, pulled down the blinds and refused to leave his bed all week.

Another of the patients I observed was Frieda, a double-jointed steno near my room 310. She was a yeller, a tray-thrower, and general cut-up. Her illness was run of the mill and consequently not very dramatic, but that didn't cramp Frieda. She was a 230-volt electric shock in a 110-volt wall socket, and the air around her even when she slept had the smell of a short circuit.

Of course, I had many moments when I was alone with nothing to do except look out the window. Some of these completely idle moments were the best of the day. Because of them, for instance, I knew all about the little boy across the street who, for six months, tried to learn to crack a bull whip. Every week or so the whip would backfire and bite off a piece of him, and he would howl bloody murder and his mother would arrive with iodine. A few days later he would be out trying it again.

Slowly I trained myself not to think depressing thoughts. I changed papers to avoid any comments that I could not stand. I became an addict of comic strips, crossword puzzles and how to make pineapple crumpets. In the matter of books I found that biography and history are by all odds the safest fare and the most instructive. The troubles of the past did not lead my thoughts in depressing channels, and they corrected a too dreary attitude towards the troubles of the present. Current masterpieces of social significance could be read at some future date when I was completely well.

Like everybody else I had my pets among hospital personnel. For instance, there were the pinkies or probies, in their pink uniforms.

These three-year students on their way to registered nurse certificates were as busy as a three-ring circus, especially the brand-new pinkies who had never seen a thermometer before. Most of the patients on my floor did not need expert care and that is why the new pinkies were turned loose to practice on us. I will always remember these first meetings. A strange knock on the door, then the new pinkie approached, timid or truculent or excruciatingly blasé. A fellow never knew what notions would be in her head but he could be sure that the older pinkies and nurses had loaded it with eyewash. Apparently I was represented as a) Harpo Marx, b) a Greek sponge diver or c) a dangerous roué to be kept at a safe distance to avoid sexual harrassment or d) God knows what else.

I had spells of trying to trick nurses and doctors, orderlies, and cleaning girls into statements out of which I could concoct a prognosis. People like me are to blame for the maddening wariness of doctors. I remember saying to my orderly, Frank Smentowski, "Those first-floor patients are all in pretty good shape, aren't they?" "Pretty good," Frank would say. Then I would add, "Must be some real sick ones on this floor, uh, Frank?" "A few maybe." "I guess they put all the worse cases on this floor, don't they?" Frank gave me a funny look. "You dumb cluck," he said, "what's the use of stewing? You don't need a doc. All you need is somebody to tell you what not to think about."

I thought about Frank's remark about what not to think about, how to keep ourselves from wrestling with self-pity. I concluded that self-pity plagued people because they wouldn't accept facts and get on with the business of getting well. Failure to accept facts seemed to be ten times worse than the facts themselves, and facts must be swallowed eventually anyhow. But I would worry anyway, and I would slowly sink up to my ears in a muck of self-reproach. Every fool thing I had ever done, every shabby act, every failure, every time I went out and got drunk and did something ridiculous would parade across my counterpane. I knew that some of us had only ourselves to blame when we landed in hospitals. But I thought that this payoff of illness was usually a heavier penalty than our sins warranted. For everyone who broke down ninety-nine other people equally bruised went their cock-eyed way unscathed. They escaped illness because they had better physical resistance, not stronger or more beautiful characters.

One of the enduring interests I developed in my curing period was bird watching. This because Dr. Webb was an avid bird watcher and liked to share his interest. He encouraged me to put a feeding platform outside my bedroom window. Later EJ and I drove for miles looking at birds. It became a favorite pastime of ours that has persisted to this day.

More than anything else while I was in the hospital I enjoyed the twice-daily visits of my beloved Edna Jane. I could always recognize the sound of her heels clicking down the corridor as she came to report how the children were and whatever happened to her day by day.

Chapter Twenty-Five

THE BLESSINGS OF ILLNESS

D R. WEBB believed that a patient on bed rest reaches a stage of
TB that doctors call "an arrested case." I had gained twenty-
five pounds during that bed rest period. Dr. Webb allowed me to at
least get out of bed and make a little jaunt to the beautiful city park of
Colorado Springs called Austin Bluffs where we would have lunch at
one of the picnic areas and practice my new hobby of bird watching. I
was just beginning and of course, I called the birds I saw by the wrong
names for a while. I even began to do a little writing of publicity for
the Red Cross's annual fund drive.

With my improved status as an arrested case, Dr. Webb had released me from strict bed rest and let me have callers.

One day my nurse gave me a look suggesting I was in for a bad time
and brought in a caller. "This is Miss Eliza Carlisle," she said. "You
are on her church list." Somehow I expected a tall female with a stern
face, huge feet in blockbuster shoes. Instead, Miss Carlisle was barely
four feet high. She wore a tiny black hat with lilies of the valley all
over it. She was obviously the sort of lady who wrapped blankets in
tissue paper before putting them away for the winter. She stepped toward me stripping a white glove from her tiny hand, "I'm Miss Carlisle
of the well-known Carlisles from Ashtabula. That's in Ohio, you know.
I'm one of those awful bats the Episcopalians send out to bore hospital
patients to death." She explained that she had come to Glockner in
1913 when Dr. Webb's colleague Dr. Charles Fox Gardiner had "sani-
tary" tents put out in the hospital grounds with flocks of nuns scurry-

ing in and out of the tents to attend to their needs. "They kept us in those tents well into winter though we nearly froze to death. They thought that would cure us. Well, it did. I got well and moved into my eighties. So carry on. You will, too." With that my caller patted my hand and was gone.

I especially enjoyed the visits of Dr. Webb's daughter Marka. She told me that her father had come to Colorado Springs from Guy's Hospital in London. He had built up a large practice treating tuberculars at the turn of the century at Glockner. During World War I, General Pershing appointed Dr. Webb to set up four TB hospitals for American soldiers who came down with TB in France and to tour them regularly to see that they were managed properly. She said, "But his main interest is in finding a drug to cure or kill the TB germ." The back part of his house on Cascade Avenue was full of monkeys, rabbits and white mice for experimental inoculation by his assistants, who included a bacteriologist that he brought to Colorado Springs from Holland, Dr. Charles Boissevain. Dr. Webb did not find the drug but the work he began is carried on today by the Webb-Waring Tuberculosis Research Institute associated with the University of Denver. Today it is the most important foundation in the United States for research on tuberculosis. It is funded in part by money contributed to Dr. Webb for his lab in Colorado Springs given to him by grateful TB patients.

Marka also told me that her father had married Varina Davis, a granddaughter of the president of the Confederacy, Jefferson Davis.

Two visitors sent to me by Marka were Broadmoor ex-TBs who had chased the cure first at the famous TB sanitarium in Davos, Switzerland. They were two charming ladies, Merrily Duncan and Romaine Lilly. When their doctor there, Alexius Forster, left to manage Cragmoor Sanitarium, they followed him. They said that Dr. Forster believed strongly that romance helped patients recover from TB along with bed rest and plenty of fresh air. He ran telephone lines from all his male patients to the beds of female patients so that their love could bloom via their telephones. He started a weekly newspaper *Ninety-eight-six* written by the patients. A letters to the editor column allowed the lovelorn to express their feelings. Dr. Forster, they said, was a fresh air fiend requiring everyone to wear scanty clothes which encouraged romance. Both ladies had found their husbands while chasing the cure at Cragmoor.

One never-to-be forgotten day, I heard somebody tapping on my door. The door opened and a smallish man entered. He walked timidly toward my bed with outstretched hand to shake mine. "My name," he said softly, "is Vincent Youmans." I sat up in bed and almost screamed, "Vincent Youmans! The great song writer? I can't believe it." He said, "My friend Marka asked me to stop by. Her father has been my TB doctor for a dozen years, but I am afraid I have not been a very good patient. I have played all my songs for Marka even before they were published." I said, "Oh, my Lord, Vincent. Our little Princeton jazz band played your tunes on Tourist Third because the dancers demanded them over and over—'Tea for Two,' 'Sometimes I'm Happy,' 'I Know That You Know,' and that beautiful ballad, 'Through the Years.' You know, Vincent, you will be ranked forever with Jerome Kern, George Gershwin and Cole Porter." He smiled shyly. "How nice of you." He rose. "I have to go to Denver. Goodby and good luck." And he was gone. Hallelujah!

In 1946, Vincent Youmans, the son of a New York hatter, died of tuberculosis in a Denver hospital at the age of forty-eight. As I had done when George Gershwin died, I wept.

———

There's more to a long illness than mere time passing. As I look back over my two years and speculate what I would have done with that time if I had not fallen ill, I have to conclude that that time couldn't have been spent more constructively. This is not to imply that a long illness in bed creates a superior being. I don't believe as one great philosopher that no man should be elected to high public office until he has spent so many hours in bed. Invalids have risen to greatness, but so have those who have lived and died without ever experiencing the supreme indignity of mounting that chilly and desolate promontory, the bedpan. Furthermore, most of the lessons of invalidism are soon forgotten by those who have received them.

But there is one lesson that seems to stick. When a fellow lies in bed month after month, he begins to see with blinding clarity what is and what is not important to him. The illness process, with its moments of heightened perception, has the same drastic effect on sick people that a threshing machine has on a shock of wheat on the farm.

Before I got TB I behaved much like our cocker spaniel who had so many interests around the yard, so many bones and smelling stations, that she was in a perpetual froth trying to keep her mind on all of them. I hadn't been in bed more than a month before I began to understand that both dogs and men are severely restricted in the number of bones they can attend to properly.

And so it happened that when I got well finally I trimmed down my interests to a volume that I could handle. Goodness knows how long it would have taken me to do that if I hadn't got sick. Long illness, therefore, provided me with a short cut to a simplified view of life, to a weeding out of fruitless nonsense and disillusioning aspiration that would have exhausted me and made me wind up empty-handed. The perceptions of an invalid, I must say, have a lot in common with those of an octogenarian. Sick people and old people are perfectly aware that nothing much matters but love and bread and little glass beads. It makes no difference whether the beads come from Tiffany's or Woolworth's as long as they catch the sun.

And so way back there in Glockner Hospital, I came to the conclusion that one should not regard illness as an abnormal period of mental and physical stagnation. Instead, it paves the way to a saner employment of this peculiar energy stuff called life. And so I found that that wonderful instrument we all have, the mind, prevented me from being confined. My mind gave me the whole universe spreading within the vast limits of my own head.

The purpose of long illness, of course, is recovery. We go to bed in various stages of disrepair. Naturally we have to cope with low periods when we suspect that all the things we love may be fading away for us. We are bound to have these spells, but the time comes in long illness when we know we are getting well! So what of these dreary days of confinement? Is the path dreary to the foot of the rainbow?

Chapter Twenty-Six

MONEY MOUNTAIN

I N SEPTEMBER 1947 Dr. Webb told me that my x-rays showed that the inch-long cavity in my left lung had healed completely, and I was cured of my tuberculosis at last. We played a game of chess that afternoon in celebration, and he beat me with a king's pawn opening and then brought me a double jigger scotch and soda to ease the pain of my chess loss.

Dr. Webb had introduced me to many people at Glockner, but the one I enjoyed talking to most was a colleague of his, Dr. Charles Fox Gardiner. Dr. Gardiner told me that he had gone to Paris when he was twelve years old in 1872, which was the year that Gustav Courbet and his followers pulled down the Vendome Column, a symbol of the regime of Napoleon Bonaparte III. Dr. Gardiner told me that he had taken his medical training at Bellevue Hospital in New York City. Going west, seeking adventure, he had begun practice in the small Western slope village of Meeker, Colorado. His neighbors in Meeker were such a healthy lot that he had to earn his keep by treating the tumors of their mules.

One of his patients was the wife of a rancher who lived a few miles out of Meeker. Dr. Gardiner knew that the wife of that rancher was due to have a baby on a certain date. So he saddled up his pony on a bitterly cold winter day and rode through a snowstorm to the home of the wife. Her home was cold, and he could find no wood to start a fire. He delivered the baby and then there was nothing to do but put the mother and baby in bed, pile comforters on them, then climb in beside the mother to add his warmth to theirs against the cold. In the morning, the rancher returned with firewood and found his wife and baby in bed with her doctor, all comfortable and warm. He was so pleased with the successful birth that he paid Dr. Gardiner the usual fee for delivering a baby or a heifer calf, then gave him a second heifer calf for his good work. As Dr. Gardiner wrote in his entertaining autobiography titled *Doctor at Timberline,* "I am sure that I was probably the only doctor in Colorado who ever received the present of a calf from the father of a baby for sleeping with his wife."

Dr. Gardiner left Meeker in 1913 to join Dr. Webb in practice at Glockner Hospital. He told me that during the 1890s he went often to Cripple Creek to see what was going on during the Cripple Creek gold rush during which that gold camp was the richest in the world. In the 1890s the Western Federation of Miners at Cripple Creek seized Bull Hill which contained the richest gold mines of the district and demanded of their owners in Colorado Springs a $3.00 a day minimum wage. The Colorado Springs mine owners led by President William Slocum of Colorado College organized an army of deputy sheriffs and sent them to Cripple Creek to recover Bull Hill from the miners. They hired Dr. Gardiner to accompany the army in case there was bloodshed in the battle. The battle did not occur as the deputy sheriffs, according to Sheriff Bowers, marched up Bull Hill and saw the miners guns pointed at them and hurriedly marched back down again.

Dr. Gardiner's Cripple Creek stories fascinated me. I asked him, "Could you bring me a history of the Cripple Creek District?" "No," Dr. Gardiner said, "No history has ever been written." "Well," I told him, "if Dr. Webb gets me on my feet, I will write a history of Cripple Creek." And so I got myself down to work in 1950 at home. I was allowed to bring home files of the *Colorado Springs Gazette* which had maintained a reporter at Cripple Creek to report daily the goings on up there. I read all those reports for the ten-year boom period and wrote the book from them, mostly in bed. I did not have the slightest idea how a history should be written, but I decided that I would write about the events as though I were writing a feature story.

I spent six months writing the book and sent it off to Carl Brandt with the title *Money Mountain.* In a week or so I received a letter from Brandt and Brandt's book expert, Bernice Baumgarten. (Bernice was married to the fine novelist James Gould Couzens.) Her letter said briefly, "You have written an interesting book, Marshall, but you have so many people involved in the story that I can't keep them apart in my mind. Could you simplify them a bit?" Well, I was not happy, but I knew that Bernice Baumgarten knew what she was talking about. I decided to rewrite the book and confine the Cripple Creek action to a dozen main characters such as Spencer Penrose, the millionaire carpenter Stratton, and the plumber Jimmie Burns, whose mines had brought them large fortunes in the millions of dollars.

After I sent Bernice the rewritten version, I told her that I had just been reading an article in the July 1951 issue of the new travel magazine *Holiday* about Cripple Creek written by Robert M. Coates who wrote articles for *The New Yorker Magazine*. His article had said that he had spent a year of his boyhood in Cripple Creek, and the piece dealt with his recollections as they might relate to the gold rush that was occurring in Cripple Creek at that time.

Bernice sent the galleys of my rewritten *Money Mountain* to John Woodburn who was the New York editor of the Boston publisher Little, Brown and Company. It had already been turned down by Alfred Knopf and McGraw Hill, but Woodburn happened to be having lunch with Coates the day he got the galleys, and he went to luncheon with the galleys under his arm and loaned them to Coates to read which he did. He reported back to John Woodburn that it was a book that he wished he had written. It was a good account of all the excitement at Cripple Creek, he said. John Woodburn reported back to Bernice, then wrote me the very next day saying that Little, Brown would publish *Money Mountain* soon.

You can imagine the excitement that Woodburn's letter of acceptance of *Money Mountain* was to Edna Jane and to me. A much greater thrill came to us when the published book arrived in the spring of 1953. It was a beautiful publishing job with a big picture of me on the back of the jacket and a good photograph of Cripple Creek town on the front of the jacket. My bookseller friend in Colorado Springs, Edith Farnsworth, had an autograph party for the book at the Antlers Hotel. She hired an entertainer, Pete LaFarge (the son of Oliver LaFarge, whose book on Indians in New Mexico had won a Pulitzer Prize) to strum the guitar for those attending.

Money Mountain, I was astonished to find out, received quite good reviews in *The New York Times* and many other papers. It was also promoted well by Jack Foster, the editor of the *Rocky Mountain News* in Denver. I think that Little, Brown's first edition of *Money Mountain,* which totaled about ten thousand copies, sold out that summer, and a second edition of the hardback was printed with fourteen more editions to follow over the years. And so *Money Mountain* was an original success, although not to be compared in any way with the true best sellers. It never was a best seller, but it did cover the cost of printing it even before it went on sale and continued selling on and on through the years. Even forty years later I see, by a recent royalty statement from the University of Nebraska Press who reprinted it, that there have been four paperback editions.

I will not try to explain why *Money Mountain* sold so well in this modest way except to say that it showed that people the world over like to read about people striking it very rich. Of course, gold mining engineers all the world over, England, Australia, South Africa and the United States, and the relatives of people who invested in gold mines, bought the book through all those years. I hope they will keep buying it into the next century.

My only regret about the pleasure of writing *Money Mountain* and seeing it published was that our beloved Dr. Webb did not live long enough to read it. He died on January 27, 1948 at his Cascade Avenue house of a heart attack.

Chapter Twenty-Seven

AMERICA THE BEAUTIFUL

EDNA JANE and I were pleased at the success of *Money Mountain* although we were saddened when word came that another of our special people had died. John Woodburn who had bought the book from me for Little, Brown and Co. died unexpectedly and never saw the book reach the bookstores. I went to New York from Colorado Springs to meet the new New York editor of Little, Brown and Co. whose name was Ned Bradford. I liked Bradford on sight. He urged me to come up with an idea for another book on Western history and said that Little, Brown was ready to publish if I wrote it.

Meanwhile, during that summer I wrote several magazine articles for *True Magazine, American Mercury* and others. The magazine articles paid well, but Bernice Baumgarten advised me to stick to writing books because magazine articles were so ephemeral. Books, she said, would be bought by libraries and would be read by people with real and lasting interest.

As I considered subjects for a second book with Ned Bradford, I thought of the Nathan Meeker story. I was following a plan of trying to write on subjects that had not been fully covered before. I was also attracted to the man, Nathan Meeker, who had been a newspaper reporter for Horace Greeley's *New York Herald* and who came to Colorado with others and started the Union Colony, a cooperative and temperance colony, on the site of the town of Greeley, Colorado. They picked Greeley after looking at the site of Colorado Springs which did not have sufficient water supply. EJ was enthusiastic about writing the

Meeker story because it took place on a fine trout stream, the White River. So we went there and did research beginning at the little stream Milk Creek where the U.S. Army troops met the Utes when they came from Wyoming to rescue the murdered Nathan Meeker's wife and daughter Josie who were held captive by the Utes for several weeks. They were both raped.

I sent the galleys of *Massacre: the Tragedy at White River* to Hugh Kaylor who had found a new career as fiction editor of the *Ladies Home Journal*. I was hoping wistfully that he might find a section of it that the *Journal* might use. Hugh sent back the galley with a note, "*Massacre* is a powerful story, Marsh, but you know nobody gets raped in the *Ladies Home Journal*." *Massacre* was published by Little, Brown in 1957 and sold moderately well even into the 1990s.

I had long since decided that I could not write a single line without first going to see the place I was writing about—first, because I could write about it better, but second, because of the sheer pleasure of travel in our wonderful western country. In our traveling for the Meeker story we had crossed several Rocky Mountain passes and I realized there was no book about passes. So I decided to write a book for Little, Brown on the history of the Rocky Mountain passes. Most were crossed for economic reasons; mining was an important factor. Roads were built later for automobile tourists and before that railroads crossed the passes to get to the West Coast. The history of those passes would present a pretty good survey of the economic development of the West. I decided to call the book *The Great Gates*.

I got started and gradually moved up out of Colorado to cover the rest of the Rockies, northward into Wyoming and Montana and then into the Canadian Rockies as far as Jasper, Manitoba. The highest mountain, Mount Robeson out of Jasper over Yellowhead Pass, was the highest Canadian peak and was only 12,972 feet. For some reason I got stuck midway, as every book writer knows can happen, in writing *The Great Gates*. I told a Denver publisher friend of mine, Alan Swallow, how I was behind in writing *The Great Gates*. He said, "Why don't you take off a year and write a history of Colorado Springs?" So I got permission from Little, Brown to delay the contract date on the passes book and spent a year writing *Newport in the Rockies*. The name was a sort of joke but it seemed like a good idea to give Colorado Springs the name of the famous fashionable resort back east. Alan Swallow agreed and actually the *Newport* title did give the town a certain quality. To this day some of the real estate developments in Colorado Springs have the name Newport attached to them.

I was surprised that *Newport* did not sell badly even though books about towns often do. It did all right because the main characters, General William Jackson Palmer, who started the town, and Spencer Penrose, who built the Broadmoor Hotel to make the town a very successful resort, were very dynamic and colorful characters. Another interesting character was Count James Pourtales, a German nobleman who developed the Broadmoor area as residential project. *Newport in the Rockies: The Life and Times of Colorado Springs* was published in 1961.

———

EJ and I crossed all the high passes of Colorado including the highest, such as Mosquito Pass above Leadville at thirteen thousand feet above sea level. EJ did most of the driving of our little 1949 Army jeep. She sat steady at the wheel on those dangerous shelf roads with drops of more than two thousand feet off the road. I sat as far outside as I could so I could jump out of the jeep if we should fall.

The passes book was written in 1964 and sold quite well until it went out of print in the 1980s. Of course, EJ was wildly enthusiastic about researching the passes because streams cut most passes, and those streams are full of trout.

After the passes book I wrote, for Ned Bradford, *So Vast, So Beautiful a Land* about the Louisiana Purchase. Researching it we drove at least ten thousand miles. We drove to Montreal, then while we were at it on to Nova Scotia, down the St. Lawrence as LaSalle had gone. Then another year we went to the beautiful country in northern Michigan and crossed Lake Michigan to Green Bay, drove down the Fox River to Wisconsin through Peoria where we camped where LaSalle had camped once in Heartbreak Camp on his way with Hennepin to discover the Mississippi. We did research in the excellent library at the Minnesota Historical Society.

After five years of hard work and research I finished writing my history of the Louisiana Purchase. Of course, many other people have written about Thomas Jefferson's incredibly wonderful act on behalf of the United States in making it a continental power by acquiring that land that otherwise would be a part of France today with the Mississippi. But I'll bet I'm the only one who drove or walked every inch of it.

We both thought that *So Vast* was my best book. Little, Brown published it in 1974, a beautiful publishing job with wonderful maps of the various stages of the development of the land of the Louisiana Purchase. I was delighted in 1990 when the Ohio University Press, which had been the publisher of *Newport in the Rockies* for many years after Alan Swallow's death, decided to reprint *So Vast, So Beautiful a Land* exactly as it was printed originally in 1975 by Little, Brown.

In 1976 I was asked by the National Endowment for the Humanities to write one of its fifty-two state histories that it published in 1976 in honor of the bicentennial of the Declaration of Independence. So I wrote *Colorado* that year. We had fun researching the flat side of Colorado—the eastern side.

In all our thousands of miles of research EJ and I had surprisingly few mishaps. Once on top of Ellwood Pass at thirteen thousand feet we got the jeep stuck in a pot hole. A couple of suspicious prospectors, who thought we were spying on their search for a bonanza, pulled us out grumpily. We mollified them with nips from our bottle of Scotch.

Another time we went up to Yellowstone in the fall to see the golden aspen. Early one morning in the motel I heard someone yelling, "Hey, Colorado! There's a bear in your car." I stepped out and saw a mother bear sitting in the middle seat eating our picnic goodies while her cubs watched from the outside. I kept a discreet distance because bears are notoriously protective of cubs, but I yelled and she crawled out and ambled away, followed by the cubs. Later I was able to collect insurance on their scratches on the upholstery. On the advice of my agent I put in a claim citing malicious mischief!

I will conclude this book with a mention of our years in the present city of Colorado Springs which has grown very much during our time there. When we arrived in 1941 it had a population of thirty thousand. With the coming of Fort Carson, the North American Defense Command, the Air Force Academy, Peterson Field and a whole bunch of computer companies, it is now around four hundred thousand.

In 1963 we bought a small ranch in the mountains west of Colorado Springs and built a fishing cabin near a stream where EJ fishes a great deal in summers for trout, rainbow, brown, brook and occasional cutthroat. I pass my time watching the many birds up there which included those most beautiful of Western birds, Western tanagers. We never know when we will be astonished to see some strange bird. One day I saw a bittern. In winter we occasionally see flocks of rosy finches, amazingly hardy little birds. We see sora rails, snipe, killdeers, of course. We have one resident eagle and an occasional marsh hawk and red-tailed hawk. Also spectacular yellow-headed blackbirds. So that is fun, but of course, I spent most of my time in my office in Colorado Springs writing my books of Western history which EJ so beautifully edits for me. The books are really hers as much as mine.

Once there was a professor from Wellesley College who spent a summer in Colorado Springs giving a course in English at Colorado College. Her name was Katherine Lee Bates. She was an adventurous type and decided to ride the cog train to the top of Pikes Peak. As she stood at the top she took in the overwhelming view: 120 miles westward to Mt. Princeton, 75 miles northward to Mt. Evans above Denver, and southward to Mt. Blanca, eastward nearly to Kansas.

Inspired by the experience she wrote the words which became the lyrics of a song, "America the Beautiful," set to music by a Boston friend of hers Samuel A. Ward. Of course it has become the most popular patriotic hymn sung at least as often as "The Star Spangled Banner" (and certainly more singable!).

After our years of travel in this country, border to border, EJ and I had to conclude that Katharine Lee Bates was right. The United States with its incredible variety of scene is the most beautiful country. We vowed to do whatever we could to keep it that way.

So long, Oolong!

Acknowledgements

I AM INDEBTED to John Sheridan, head librarian, and all the others at Colorado College's Tutt Library where I researched events described in my book.

My thanks go to Kingsley Hubby, daughter of my dear friends Mr. and Mrs. Hugh Kahler, who recalled my visits with the Kahlers and how her father tried to teach me the writing style he used in producing more than two hundred short stories for *The Saturday Evening Post*.

When my eyesight faded, my friend and typist Barbara Neilon faithfully transcribed my book from cassettes, deleting profanity and repetitions.

I wish to thank my literary agent Carl D. Brandt, and before him his father, who pushed me for sixty years to produce my books. The work has brought me great pleasure, some despair and an occasional small triumph.

Finally, I wish to thank my family for their support. My sons Joseph and Stephen Sprague and my daughter Sharon have all been a constant source of strength and happiness as have my sister, Josephine Taylor, and my wife, Edna Jane.

May 1994   Marshall Sprague
Colorado Springs, Colorado

Index

Magnus, Helen (see Sprague)
Markel, Lester, 130
Meeker, Nathan, 157–58
Miller, Fleek, 26
Minovitz, Borah, 126
Moore, Grace, 126
Moss, Arthur, 114
Moundbuilders Country Club, 11–12
Murphy, Robert, 115, 117

Newark, Ohio, 1; history of, 2
New York Times, 130–31
Norris, Charles G., 13, 127, 132–34
Norris, Kathleen, 127, 132–34
North China Star, 5, 101, 103–9

O'Flaherty, Liam, 137
O'Hara, John, 125
Ohio and Erie Canal, 2
Osburn, James, 4, 15–17
Osburn, Louisa (grandmother), 4, 15–16, 84

Palmer, Gen. William Jackson, 159
Paris Herald, 111–29
Paul, Elliot, 112
Penrose, Spencer, 155
Phelps, William Lyon, 127
Pond, Chester, 29
Pons, Lily, 125
Pourtales, Count James, 159
Princeton University, 1, 41–48, 55–59, 68–70, 74–79

Rachmaninoff, Sergei, 125
Reese, Everett D., 131, 137
Rickenbacker, Edward, 126
Robertson, Sparrow, 113
Russell, Bertrand, 126
Russell, Hamilton, 115, 138
Ruth, Babe, 125–26

Shenk, Allen, 39–43, 55–59, 68, 74
Shenk, Chick, 39–43, 55–59, 68, 74, 88
Shirer, William, 120

Smentowski, Frank, 143, 146–47
Snyder, Mrs. Roy, 70
Snyder, Roy, 70
Sprague, Della Grace Cochran (mother), 3–4, 6, 11, 13, 15, 18–22, 24, 26–27, 37, 52–53, 86
Sprague, Edna Jane Ailes (wife), 19–20, 70–73, 75–77, 85, 87–88, 136–40, 143–44, 159–70
Sprague, Elizabeth Taylor (grandmother), 2
Sprague, Fanny (aunt), 2, 6, 12
Sprague, George (uncle), 2–3, 5–6
Sprague Grocery Company, 3, 72
Sprague, Helen Magnus, 39
Sprague, Henry Day (grandfather), 2, 84
Sprague, Henry (uncle), 2–3, 33, 36–37, 38–39, 48
Sprague, Henry H. II, 39
Sprague, Joseph Taylor (father), 2–4, 7, 10–11, 13–14, 18–19, 26–27, 33, 38, 77, 79, 83
Sprague, Joseph Taylor II (son), 138, 143
Sprague, Mary Aplin (aunt), 2–10, 77, 79, 84
Sprague, Stephen John Eugene (son), 144
Stein, Gertrude, 119
Stewart, Mrs. John Wolcott (Marka), 150
Swallow, Alan, 160

Tarkington, Booth, 89
Taylor, Erik, 97, 102, 130, 136
Taylor, Howard, 36–37, 66, 90, 96, 97–100, 102, 130
Taylor, Josephine Taylor Sprague (sister), 1, 5, 7, 12, 36–37, 66, 90, 96–97, 102, 130–31, 133, 136–37, 140
Thompson, Dorothy, 120
Thompson, Tommy, 113–15, 117–27
Tientsin, 97–109
Tiger, Vera, 143